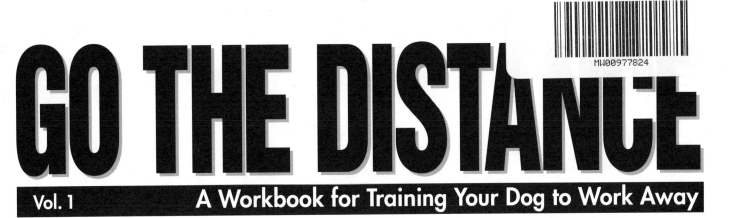

GO THE DISTANCE

Vol. 1   **A Workbook for Training Your Dog to Work Away**

by Bud Houston & Stacy Peardot

with Appendixes by Linda Mecklenburg

Clean Run Productions LLC

35 Walnut Street, Turners Falls, MA 01376

INTRO

Go the Distance

Published by   **Clean Run Productions, LLC**
35 Walnut Street
Turners Falls, MA 01376
(800) 311-6503 or (413) 863-9243
www.cleanrun.com

Editors   Betsey Lynch, Linda Mecklenburg, Monica Percival, and Marcille Ripperton
Cover Design   Chris Parker, Speedoggie Graphix
Book Design and Typesetting   Monica Percival
Cover Photos   Copyright © 1999 Skipper Productions
Book Illustrations   Chris Lewis Brown, Roger Brucker, Bob Ebdon, Karen Gaydos, Cherie Gessford, Jim Liddle, Jo Ann Mather, Nancy Krouse-Culley, and Valerie Pietraszewska.
Printing   Hadley Printing Company

ISBN 1-892694-01-8

Contents

Program Director's Notes

This workbook represents an eight-week training program for distance work in dog agility. It is an *example* of a curriculum, somewhat introductory in nature, and well-balanced in its presentation. It is our intention to introduce distance training, to make clear the objectives, to provide lesson plans, and to start our intrepid readers in the right direction. The exercises and discussions here are intended for the instructors of the training program. Pages are included that are suitable for handout material for the students in the program.

Objectives of This Distance Program

Teaching a dog to work at a distance is an enormous training feat, which encompasses dozens of skills and nuances. The agility team must be devoted students.

A balanced training program addresses different at-a-distance styles. One style might be committed to complex directionals and discrimination skills. Another style might revolve around relative directionals and handler motion cues. The training program should provide a format for exercising and proofing, while introducing your students to each of the different styles and accommodating any difference in style.

About the Logistics of a Training Program

The presentation in this workbook may appear to suggest or endorse the one right way to conduct a distance training program. However, training programs for dog agility take a variety of forms. Programs differ in terms of basic training techniques, administration, length of program, and guidelines for admittance and graduation.

Guidelines for Admittance

Training for distance in dog agility presupposes that the dog has a variety of skills, indicating that the dog is prepared for more advanced training. This is *not* fare for a green dog, young dog, or any dog new to agility.

The bare-bones guidelines for admittance should include:

- The dog should be a motivated and happy worker. Distance work requires sufficient confidence in the dog to leave his handler's side. The dog should also be competing in agility and his running time in standard agility classes should be under standard course time (SCT). It is unlikely that a dog that cannot work at an acceptable speed at the handler's side will do so at a distance from the handler.

- A completed class application and prepayment of the training fee. Prior to the first class, the dog's owner should submit an application for enrollment. This application should include the owner's signature, a release of liability, and proof of current vaccinations. Be sure that you have a clearly stated policy regarding refunds (if any) for cancellation.

What Your Students Should Bring to Class

When you confirm a dog's enrollment in your training program, use the opportunity to remind your students what they need to bring to class. Here's a good list for you to work with:

- A buckle collar or a quick release collar.

- A 4" or 6" tab lead.

- A 6' obedience lead.

- Lots of the dog's favorite food treats contained either in a bait bag or a food tube.

- A toy motivator (such as a ball, a Frisbee™, or a squeaky toy).

- Water and a bowl for the dog.

How to Divide Your Classes

Most classes in this workbook have three or four working "sets". A set is the collection of equipment for which one instructor is responsible in the course of the class. It is usually better, though certainly not required, for one instructor to remain with the same set of equipment throughout the class, while the students, divided into groups, switch off between sets during the class. Divide your class evenly, one group of students for each set.

The sets are intended be worked simultaneously by a large class; or consecutively by a small class. If you are working with simultaneous sets, it is necessary to divide your students into logical groups. The best way to divide a class is by jump height. This allows dogs of the same jump height to work together, so not a lot of time is spent adjusting bars.

NOTE: Throughout this workbook we make reference to "big dogs" and "little dogs". In general, any dog that measures 16" or less at the shoulders is considered a little dog. Any dog measuring more than 16" is a big dog.

Another way to divide a class is by skill level. For example, if you use the data on the Progress Worksheets in this book to group together the dogs having difficulty with certain skills, it will be possible to fashion a more remedial program for just those dogs. Dogs that are advancing more quickly can be given a more advanced program.

If you divide your class into several groups, the time that students spend on each set should be carefully monitored; otherwise it is possible that there will not be time to get to all the required sets. To make this work, one of your instructors must be assigned the task of keeping time. If there are four sets and four groups of students, for example, an hour should be divided into 15-minute working periods. The timekeeper will give a two-minute warning prior to each switch between sets. At the end of the 15 minutes, the timer needs to announce clearly that it is time to switch.

Setting Up for Class

From day one, be an advocate for teaching your students the proper work ethic for participation in this sport. Setting up equipment is a lot of work. Get your students involved. If you get them used to the idea that you're going to do everything for them, they will soon come to expect you to continue to do so. Get them used to doing a share of the work and they will always expect to do their fair share.

One possibility is to require half of the class to come 30 minutes early to help set up equipment. Require the other half of the class to stay late to put equipment away and clean up the training site. Be prepared to get tough with students who won't do their fair share of work. Make them sit out a week if they don't help with the work!

Cleaning Up After the Dogs

Encourage your students to exercise their dogs before coming to class. However, accidents are sometimes unavoidable. Your policy should be that the handler is responsible for immediately cleaning up after his dog.

You could suggest to your students that the regular meal the dog might have prior to class would best be deferred to after class. This tactic will make the dog's attention that much keener!

Not Allowed!

By policy, you should not allow:

- **Aggressive dogs.** Dogs should not exhibit aggressiveness either towards other dogs or towards people.

- **Harsh training methods.**

- **Choke chains and pinch collars.**

- **Bitches in season.** Some clubs and training facilities do not allow bitches in heat. Other can function adequately if the bitch is diapered. You'll have to make the call.

- **Barking dogs.** Of course, all dogs bark. What you are guarding against here is the dog that barks without pause or purpose. This restriction is intended to placate neighbors that would be disturbed by a constantly barking animal as well as to make sure that instructors aren't struggling to be heard over the noise.

- **Dogs that run away.** If you can't catch 'em, you can't train 'em.

Don't Forget Your Instructors

Being an instructor is sometimes a thankless job. Often instructors train other people's dogs at the expense of training their own. We advocate a policy that sets aside time and facilities for instructors to put their own dogs on the equipment.

In an ideal world, your instructors should receive financial compensation for sharing their expertise and expending time and effort in support of your training program. An unpaid instructor can soon become an unhappy instructor.

How to Use This Workbook

This workbook is divided into eight lesson plans. These lessons are designed for a two-hour class, for ten or twelve students, and at least two instructors so that your students can be divided into groups.

You'll find that many of the lesson plans are built around playing one game or another. This is completely intentional. Most games require elements of timing and strategy that are beyond the simple scope of working a dog at a distance. The games give your students an opportunity to learn and practice those elements.

You'll also find that playing a game rocks the handler out of the stern drill-and-practice mode. Many dogs do not like to be drilled. So the games format intentionally works to change the demeanor of the handler so that the dog's response to the more upbeat context facilitates learning, and helps to avoid drilling.

Each lesson plan is organized along the same lines, containing the elements described in the following sections. These pages can be copied for your students and your instructors.

Instructor Notes

This is an introduction to each weekly plan. Each begins with a frank discussion of the task of training students and dogs for distance work in agility. Your lead instructor should begin here to understand the philosophy of the training to be delivered. The "Organizational Notes" will help prepare for the weekly training program. Copies should be distributed to all instructors at least one week prior to class.

Progress Worksheets

On the back of each week's Instructor Notes is a worksheet—or if you prefer, a model for a worksheet—that is used to list all students signed up for the class, and to check them present. The Progress Worksheet includes an area to make notes about the progress of students and the difficulties a student or dog might be having with certain skills or exercises. It is very important to make good notes in order to keep track of progress and problems. The notes are a history which should be consulted by all of your instructors on a weekly basis so that you can fine tune the on-going curriculum to meet the specific needs of individual students.

Facility Layouts

The Facility Layout is a design for placement of the obstacles on your training field. Some thought has been given to the ideal placement of the obstacles in the field, considering how dogs will move through each exercise and how dogs and their handlers might line up or queue at the start of each set.

All instructors should get a copy of the Facility Layout to direct the work of setting up the equipment for the day's lesson, and to understand how exercises are worked in the context of the setup of obstacles.

Roger Brucker

Facility Layout Worksheets

In an ideal world, we all have two acres in which to set up our training sets. In the real world, however, many clubs do their training in limited spaces. It's conceivable that there won't be enough space to set up all exercises for a given week at the same time. If your agility area is smaller than the ideal field, you must design the facility layout for each week *prior* to class. For this reason, blank Facility Layout Worksheets have been provided. Feel free to make additional copies for your use.

Designing the facility layout is no small task, you will find. You have to be very thoughtful about how the obstacles are going to be set up. There should be enough room between sets so that dogs are not running into each other. This will be especially important when dogs are working off-lead. Consider too that only one dog will be working on a set at a time. You must leave room for dogs and their handlers to wait in line, and you must leave room for some kind of path for a dog finishing an exercise to get back to the end of the line.

All instructors should get a copy of the Facility Layout Worksheet, if one is used.

Weekly Exercises

Each instructor should receive a copy of *all* of the exercises for a given week. Ideally the instructors should receive their copies at least a week ahead of the scheduled class so that they can mentally prepare for what they must do with their students.

Encourage your instructors to make notes about what works and what doesn't work in the weekly training program. Your training delivery will improve by the empirical knowledge you earn while conducting classes. Instructors will develop keener eyes for training and performance issues by keeping copious notes on the process.

Student Notes

The Student Notes are to be copied and given to your students on a weekly basis. They contain work-at-home exercises, which complement and supplement the ongoing lesson plans. Most students will be avidly interested in anything they can get their hands on to read about training a dog for distance work. However, it helps to remind your students each week to actually work on the homework assignments as they are intended to increase the dog's success in class.

Your instructors should also get a copy of the Student Notes so that they understand what their students are expected to learn each week *outside* of class.

Acknowledgments

We thank all of the people who have made contributions to this workbook. A special thanks to Carole Schlaes, who tested many of our class plans, and to Linda Mecklenburg, Monica Percival and others whose distance training methodologies are reflected in the philosophy of this book. Thanks also to a wonderful corps of artists who have allowed us to use their work to brighten up these pages: Chris Lewis Brown, Roger Brucker, Bob Ebdon, Karen Gaydos, Cherie Gessford, Jim Liddle, Jo Ann Mather, Nancy Krouse-Culley, and Valerie Pietraszewska.

Roger Brucker

Practical Matters in Training Dogs for Distance

It could be that an eight-week training program is too neat a package for properly preparing dogs to work at a distance. Dogs learn at different paces. You may want to spread this training program out over a much greater span of time so that your students, and their dogs, can properly assimilate some of the skills encompassed by the curriculum. This can be accomplished in a number of ways:

- You could, for example, split up the exercises for a single week and deliver them over several weeks.

- You could give one distance class a month, which would make this an eight-month program!

- You could, on alternate weeks, simply play a Gamblers game. This would have the added benefit of testing the efficacy of the curriculum as you go along.

Many prospective students will tell you that they want to *put distance training* on their dogs. But they are not prepared to put forth the effort and commitment required to make it happen. It is not enough for a dog and handler to come to your training center once a week for an hour or two. They have to do homework. They have to be consistent. They must follow the program. This should be made very clear to prospective students. They need to understand that there is no magic. There is only hard work.

A dog that will not go away from his handler for the simplest agility task, or the dog that cannot perform agility obstacles without fault, probably is not ready for this training program. This is an advanced curriculum, intended ideally for dogs and handlers who are already comfortable working teams.

Many agility training centers do all of their work in small buildings. This is usually because these are the only facilities to which they have access. This is something of a problem when it comes to teaching a dog to work at a distance. If a training facility has a perimeter of walls to turn and direct the dogs being worked, then handlers and trainers may get a false sense of accomplishment. In practice, dogs need plenty of room to run and work in order to be trained effectively in distance work. It would be useful to occasionally take distance-training classes out to a park or some other wide-open space to really get a sense of how the dogs are doing with the curriculum.

Tracking the Progress of Students

After each week of training, sit down with your instructors to discuss the progress of your students. If you are the sole instructor, sit down and do it yourself. This will help you make important decisions about the scope and emphasis of each training session.

Besides making detailed notes about each class on your weekly Progress Worksheets, you may want to keep a consolidated worksheet for the entire eight-week class. A model for such a form is provided on page 12. It lists the major skills being taught during the program and gives you a space for recording a student's proficiency in each area for each week of the program. This will help you track overall progress.

Use any weighting system that makes sense to you. For example, you could use letter grades "A" through "F" to describe how you think a student did with the day's exercises. Also mark students "Absent" on this worksheet. This will help you correlate learning with attendance.

Make notations about your rationale for giving a grade of "C" or less to a student. Keep in mind that this is *not* so much a measurement of the student's aptitude as it is a measurement of the efficacy of the training program. Use this as intelligence to devise a game plan for giving the student exercises, homework, or training advice that will help raise the grade over the course of the program.

Index of Skills Exercises

Use the Index of Skills Exercises to identify specific exercises that can help a student with problem areas.

Handling at a Distance
- Week 1, Set 1: Proficiency Test (p. 17)
- Week 1, Set 4: Turns and Crosses (p. 20)
- Week 1, Set 5: Figure-of-Eight (p. 22)
- Week 1, Set 6: Send and Curl (p. 23)
- Week 2, Set 2: Jump-Table (p. 37)
- Week 2, Set 4: Jump 180 (p. 38)
- Week 2, Set 5: Jump, Tunnel, Jump 180 (p. 38)
- Week 2, Set 6: Jump Away, Back to the Tunnel (p. 38)
- Week 3, The Joker Training Sets: Set 7 (p. 59)
- Week 5, Set 1: Skills Review (p. 85-87)
- Week 5, Set 2: The Swimmer's Cross (p. 88)
- Week 5, Set 3: Tandem 180° (p. 89)
- Week 7, Set 1: Split Decision (p. 117)
- Week 7, Set 3: The Verelli Gambit (p. 119)
- Week 7, Student Notes: Send to Jump (p. 122)

Motivation
- Week 4, Student Notes: Tapping Mealtime Motivation (p. 77)
- Week 6, Student Notes: Toy Motivation (p. 110)

Recalls
- Week 1, Set 2: Recall Attention (p. 18)
- Week 1, Set 3: Recall Threadles (p. 19)
- Week 2, Student Notes: Leading Out (p. 42)
- Week 7, Set 4: The Calls To (p. 120)
- Week 7, Student Notes: Directed Recall (p. 122)

Handler and Dog

Skill Areas

Week 1 | Week 2 | Week 3 | Week 4 | Week 5 | Week 6 | Week 7 | Week 8

Section 1

Name:

Skill Area	Week 1	Week 2	Week 3	Week 4	Week 5	Week 6	Week 7	Week 8
Contact Obstacles & Weave Poles								
Directionals								
Discrimination								
Handling at a Distance								
Motivation								
Recalls								

Notes:

Section 2

Name:

Skill Area	Week 1	Week 2	Week 3	Week 4	Week 5	Week 6	Week 7	Week 8
Contact Obstacles & Weave Poles								
Directionals								
Discrimination								
Handling at a Distance								
Motivation								
Recalls								

Notes:

Section 3

Name:

Skill Area	Week 1	Week 2	Week 3	Week 4	Week 5	Week 6	Week 7	Week 8
Contact Obstacles & Weave Poles								
Directionals								
Discrimination								
Handling at a Distance								
Motivation								
Recalls								

Notes:

Section 4

Name:

Skill Area	Week 1	Week 2	Week 3	Week 4	Week 5	Week 6	Week 7	Week 8
Contact Obstacles & Weave Poles								
Directionals								
Discrimination								
Handling at a Distance								
Motivation								
Recalls								

Notes:

Go the Distance

Week 1: Instructor Notes

Before diving into the exciting task of distance training, you must be certain that the foundation has been laid. The following exercises have been designed to do exactly that.

Bob Ebdon

Initially, the *basic* training must be revisited and evaluated. Start by asking your students to demonstrate calling their dogs out of a distracting situation. This requires you to provide a setup. It is imperative that you are dealing with a group of dogs that will get along if a loose dog invades their space. Remind your students that an instant recall is absolutely necessary.

Also review the basic obstacle skills. Be sure that your students and their dogs understand exactly what is expected for the performance of each obstacle. Do the dogs know how to perform each obstacle independently of their handlers? Do the handlers have enough control to aid in their canine counterpart's performance at a distance?

These skills can be improved upon as training continues. It is necessary for each dog to understand basic performance skills on each of the obstacles before you ask them to negotiate the obstacles at a distance. The lesson plan for Week 1 addresses this issue with instruction for the dog in the art of independent obstacle performance.

Along with basic obedience skills and the ability to perform the obstacles properly, the dog must pay attention to the handler while working.

Attention works both ways. If a handler expects the dog to pay attention to her, she must also pay attention to the dog. It is most certainly a two way street. When a dog begins his agility-training career it is very important to institute a program that consistently rewards the dog for paying attention to the handler. This may be a food reward, toy reward, praise, or preferably, a combination.

Remind your students that their dogs were not born knowing how to direct their attention. They must learn what is the desired behavior. Through rewards and consistency you can prove to your dog that you are the greatest and most interesting thing on this planet!

Praise your students often for any improvement and remind them that it is important to lay a strong foundation to build on. These skills may take time to develop. Stick with it and the benefits will be great. These exercises are not designed for completion in one week; they may be used for training and polishing throughout the entire agility career. Enjoy these sets and think of them as the path to successful distance control and handling.

Organizational Notes

It's a good idea to start a new class with introductions all around. As your students introduce themselves, check them present on the roster. Don't forget to introduce yourself.

Call your students' attention to the homework reading and exercises. These will be supplied on a weekly basis. The weekly exercises include an eight-week lesson plan for teaching a dog *Left* and *Right* directionals.

How to Conduct the Class

Begin by playing the game Double Dog Dare Ya. This is a great game to introduce the concept of timing to your students. Timing is critical in most games of distance. The handler must develop a sense of how much time has elapsed, and have a pretty good idea of what can be accomplished in the given amount of time. Double Dog Dare Ya is described at the end of the Instructors Notes.

After the game, break your class into two or three separate groups and rotate these groups through as many of the training sets as time allows.

At the end of the class post the results for your students. They'll be interested in how they did in this training competition. It's really not important in the grand scheme of things. But it is one way to keep your students active, entertained, and engaged.

Week 1: Progress Worksheet

Instructors: **Date:**

Handler and Dog	Present	Notes

GENERAL NOTES:

Week 1: Facility Layout

One square = 10'

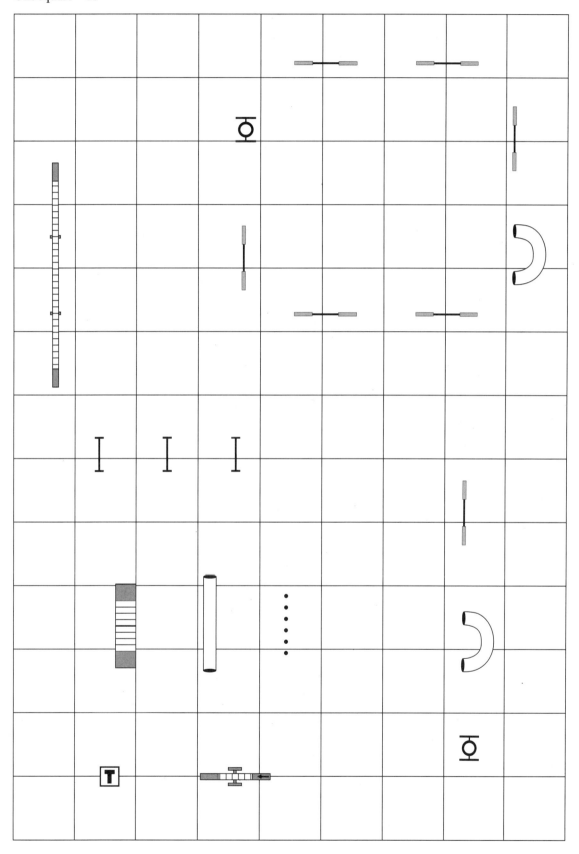

Week 1: Facility Layout Worksheet

Design your Facility Layout using a 1" = 10' scale (standard agility template)

Week 1 Exercises: The Compulsories

This lesson plan has the makings of an endless summer. These compulsory exercises probably cannot be conducted in a regular one or two-hour class. All of the exercises here should, however, be used throughout the entire eight-week session as supplementary exercises to develop and refine the basic skills required for a dog and handler team to learn to work at a distance apart.

You will find that some of your students want to teach their dogs distance work, but have in no way prepared their dogs or themselves for this kind of work. That means that many of the lessons to follow in this eight-week program will be daunting, difficult, or nearly impossible for some. You can address this difficulty solely by resorting to the repertoire of compulsory or foundation exercises outlined here.

Some of the exercises use *targeting* to aid the performance of the dog. This means that a target is placed at a strategic place at the endpoint of an exercise. The target often holds a bait or treat for the dog. Alternatively, the dog may have been trained to get a reward from his handler when he touches the target with his nose.

Sets 4 and 5 will require some equipment movement using obstacles from Set 3. Get all of your students to pitch in and help.

Set 1: Proficiency Test

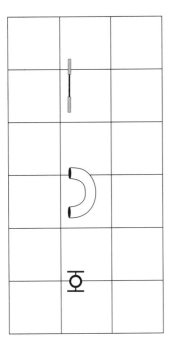

For this exercise divide your students into three groups. Each group will spend a few minutes working each obstacle, one dog and handler at a time. The objective is to determine the dog's proficiency on these three obstacles. Most obstacles can be worked in this same manner. These particular obstacles are the simplest with which to begin.

Each handler should be equipped with the dog's favorite toy, or a food tube stuffed with goodies. Have each team perform each obstacle three times, as described here, altering the starting position for each repetition.

1. Place the dog in front of the obstacle.

2. While remaining stationary, issue the verbal command for the obstacle. Once the dog commits to the obstacle, throw the reward over or through the obstacle to encourage the dog forward. In the case of the tunnel, throw the reward past the exit of the tunnel *after* the dog commits to the obstacle. This will encourage a speedy exit as well as foster commitment from the dog.

3. When the dog completes the obstacle, praise lavishly.

This exercise may be repeated as the dog begins to anticipate the throwing of the reward. The next step is to issue the command first with a slight delay in the release of the reward. This increases the criteria slightly and keeps the dog thinking.

The criteria should be gradually increased, not allowing the behavior to stagnate. The dog will learn faster if the ante is upped continually.

Set 2: Recall Attention

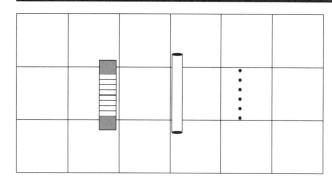

In this exercise random, full recalls are integrated into course work.

The recalls are performed in the midst of agility obstacles. The intention is to alternately ask the dog to perform an obstacle, or to come to the handler without doing an obstacle.

The dog should listen to the handler's cues and make choices accordingly. The object is to keep the dog thinking. Allow him to make the choice.

As with the majority of the exercises you will find in this workbook, the usefulness of this exercise goes beyond recall training. It also incorporates problem solving and attention.

These exercises can be great fun! Remind your students to keep those rewards coming!

Begin with the recall. Divide your students into three groups. Each group will spend a few minutes working each obstacle, one dog and handler at a time.

1. Place the dog on a stay slightly to one side or the other of the obstacle.

2. Leave the dog and go to the other end of the obstacle.

3. Turn to then face the dog.

4. Recall the dog using the dog's name and the command *Come*.

The dog should come to the handler, and ignore the adjacent obstacle. However, many dogs are already soured to a recall with obstacles present, so this may be a difficult concept for the dog to understand initially. If the dog performs the obstacle without being invited to do so, the recall should be simplified. Set the dog further away from the obstacle. The handler should also start the recall in a position closer to the dog, making it clearer to the dog what is expected.

Next, each student will do recalls, asking the dog to perform the adjacent obstacle. Perform the following steps, repeating three times for each student.

1. Place the dog on a stay slightly to one side or the other of the obstacle.

2. Leave the dog on a stay and go to the other end of the obstacle.

3. Turn to face the dog.

4. Using the dog's name and the obstacle cue, direct the dog to perform the desired obstacle.

End your training session on a positive note. Simplify this exercise, as necessary, until each dog is successful. You may have to counsel some of your students to do this kind of work as homework.

Some dogs may be so successful that you can increase the criteria. Beware of overdoing. Pushing advancement in the exercise until a dog fails would be counterproductive.

Set 3: Recall Threadles

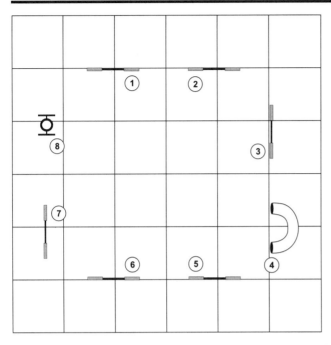

This exercise provides a practical application for the recall that your students practiced in Set 2. In a working sequence the dog is called to perform an obstacle in one instant, and then called between the obstacles in the second.

The sequence should be performed as described below.

1. Begin inside the obstacle square at jump #1.

2. Send the dog over jump #1.

3. Call the dog back, between jumps #1 and #2.

4. Send the dog over jump #3.

5. Call the dog back, between jump #3 and tunnel #4.

6. Continue around the square of obstacles in this manner, ending after a recall between jump #7 and tire #8.

After each student has gone around once, reverse direction of the exercise so that it begins with jump #2.

A handler calling the dog between obstacles should be facing the dog, indicating the obedience front position. By facing the dog the handler's entire body is a magnet of sorts, drawing the dog in. As the dog responds, the handler should praise and turn to the next obstacle, releasing the dog to perform that obstacle.

If the dog is having difficulty understanding the performance, the distance between the obstacles can be slightly increased. Also ensure that the handler's shoulders are square between the two obstacles. Turning the shoulders, even slightly, may indicate one obstacle over another. The handler should step directly backwards when calling the dog between the obstacles.

Some dogs may fail to honor the recall, coming only part way in, and then turning and taking the *next* obstacle before being told to do so. This is not acceptable. Be prepared for this possibility. Have treats available to reward the dog for coming all the way in. If the dog resists the recall, discontinue the rest of the exercise and spend time working the recall between only two jumps, praising and rewarding for small successes.

Roger Brucker

RWB

Set 4: Turns and Crosses

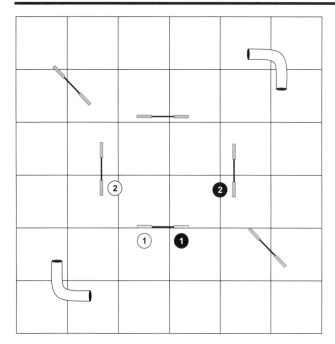

This exercise elevates the training to a much higher level of difficulty. Do *not* use directional commands in this exercise. Use the obstacle names because the dog should not take an obstacle unless directed by the handler.

This exercise requires a change of equipment.

In the first repetitions, do each of the sequences shown in the illustration in this manner:

1. With the dog on a stay, take a position between jumps #1 and #2.

2. Call the dog over jump #1.

3. As the dog commits to jump, make a 90° turn in the desired direction.

4. At the point that the dog begins to turn toward the handler, issue a second jump command to indicate jump #2.

Monitor each of your students for the timeliness of their turns and commands. Offer suggestions to improve timing. Remind your students that they must always know where the dog is in relation to the obstacle. The dog's position on the obstacle is the indicator of proper timing.

If the dog is not paying attention, the handler should turn in the *opposite* direction and say nothing. When the dog returns to the handler, give lots of praise. If the dog continues to ignore the handler's cues, a *neutral* verbal correction is necessary. Then allow the dog to try again, praising for the correct response. The verbal correction helps the dog learn his job faster. By allowing the dog to think through the problem and choose alternatives, the handler is teaching the dog to confidently try different behaviors so that he can reach the proper response himself. This commits the desired performance to memory more quickly. If the handler always provides the answer to problems, the dog will quit trying and eventually get bored. The motivated dog is the thinking dog.

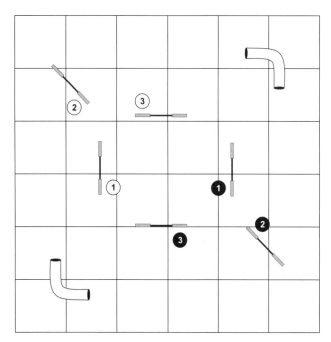

Next, front and rear crosses are added to the challenge. Each sequence can be done in two ways. Do the first repetition in this manner:

1. With the dog on a stay, take a position between jumps #1 and #2.

2. Call the dog over jump #1.

3. As the dog commits to jump, make a 90° turn in the desired direction.

4. At the point that the dog begins to turn toward the handler, issue a second jump command to indicate jump #2.

5. Cross behind the dog, and call the dog to turn toward the handler's new position.

6. As the dog turns toward the handler, command the dog to take the third jump.

Do the second repetition of each sequence in this manner:

1. Start by calling the dog over jump #1.

2. As the dog commits to jump, make a 90° turn in the desired direction.

3. At the point that the dog begins to turn toward the handler, issue a jump command to indicate jump #2.

4. Cross in front of the dog, switch lead-hands, and call the dog to turn toward the third jump.

5. As the dog turns toward the handler, command the dog to take the third jump.

Encourage your students to run a repetition, or more, silently. Omitting verbal cues from time to time in training not only tests the handler's timing and accuracy of physical cues, but also encourages the dog to pay attention. Keeping that thought in mind, be sure that your students are being consistent in their expectations and are making the challenges they present their dogs at the level at which they are working. Attention is a skill that, when learned, should offer the same rewards and consequences that any other behavior would earn. As the dog becomes more proficient in his understanding of the desired behavior, the benefits of paying attention will far outweigh the distractions.

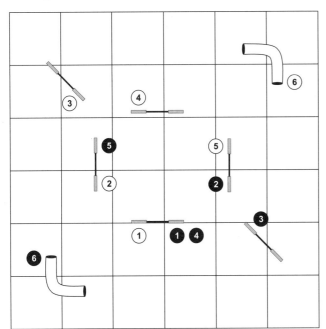

Do the final repetitions shown in this illustration. Use front or rear crosses as required.

Challenge your students to try the sequences in different ways.

Jim Liddle

Set 5: Figure-of-Eight

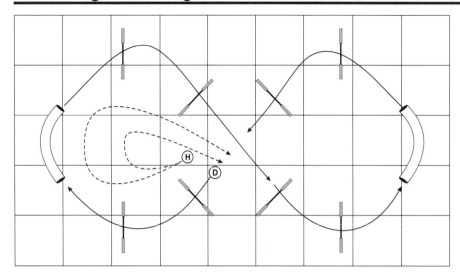

This was designed as an exercise to help a dog develop muscle tone and stamina. However, it also serves as a foundation exercise for distance work. With a greener dog the handler has to run more, staying closer to the jumps. But as the dog understands his job, the handler can lay back and take lazier inside circles.

This exercise requires a change of equipment.

Remind your students that their motion will help the dog to choose the path in front of him and go forward boldly. Don't let anyone get in the habit of slamming on the brakes while sending the dog away to do all of the work. It is the handler's obligation to know precisely how much movement is required to keep the dog in motion.

Ultimately, when the dog understands the exercise, the handler can stay back in the jump square formed at the center of the Figure-of-Eight. This allows the handler to continue to develop the basic language to communicate with the dog. *Go On* is a directional telling the dog to continue working in the present direction.

When running this exercise in class, you'll find that the point at which the handler can change sides to the dog becomes something of a puzzle. An ill-timed cross can have the handler colliding with the dog in the center of the box or pulling the dog off the curling path of the sequence. In the event that the handler can send the dog out to the exterior tunnels while remaining in the box in the center of the sequence, crossing is not really much of an issue. The handler will have plenty of leisure time to cross in front before the dog arrives.

As dogs become proficient with the basic Figure-of-Eight, you can make the figure larger, requiring the dog to run out further, as shown below. The basic objectives of the exercise remain the same. But the larger loops provide an opportunity to proof the dog's willingness to go on, and perform the obstacles in his path.

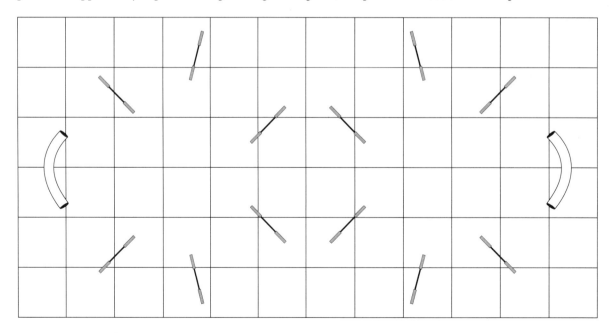

Set 6: Send and Curl

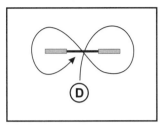

This is an exercise that demonstrates that the movement of the handler's body when working close to the dog has roughly the same effect on the dog as when dog and handler are working a distance apart.

Picture the dog doing the same jump, in the same direction, but alternately turning in different directions after jumping.

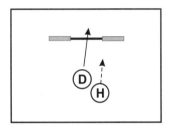

The handler's movement is, if anything, more complicated than the dog's. The exercise is basically is a series of crossing turns.

1. Start very close to the jump, working with the dog. The initial line is directly toward the jump, creating a line to the jump for the dog.

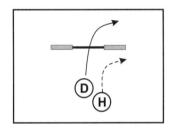

2. Curl away from the jump to influence the direction the dog will turn after making the jump.

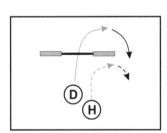

3. Start to turn away, drawing the dog back to the original side of the jump.

    Make sure that the handler doesn't take her eyes off the dog. Even when tracking away like this, the handler's attention must never leave the dog.

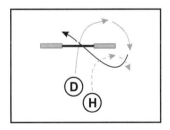

4. Next, abruptly turn back toward the dog, and push, creating a line back toward the jump.

    This action includes a change of lead-hands. The new lead-hand, sweeping up to show the new direction, is an important part of the communication between handler and dog.

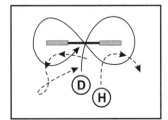

5. Repeat all of these actions for the turn in the opposite direction, and the third approach to the jump.

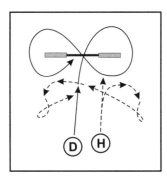

Once the dog appears to react to the lead-hand changes by the handler, the exercise can be started from a greater distance. The dog must be willing to move forward to the jump, unescorted. Using basically the same movement the handler works the dog over the jump at this increased distance.

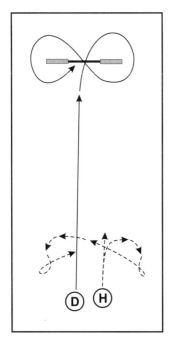

Gradually the distance from where dog and handler start, to the jump, is increased. The dog learns to work based on the handler's motion, at a considerable distance.

Set 7: Parallel on Contact

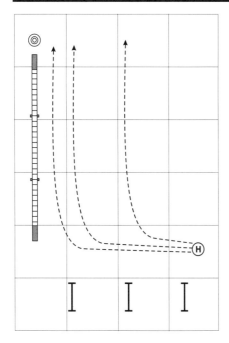

This exercise uses a baited target at the end of the dogwalk. The whole idea is that the dog learns to be comfortable completing the performance of the dogwalk at a lateral distance from his handler. The three jumps set up the turn to the dogwalk.

The handler gradually takes a lateral distance and parallel path further and further from the dog. Once the dog realizes that the target is baited he will work straight off the ramp without jumping off the side of the obstacle.

Remind the handler that although a target is present, the dog must complete the dogwalk to the specifications initially taught. This means if a stop was built into the bottom of the obstacle, it must be observed.

Consistency is always the key to continued success. The handler must be careful not to send mixed messages regarding obstacle performance while working on handling at a distance.

Set 8: Targeting the Teeter and Table

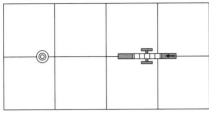

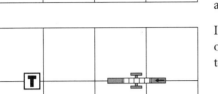

This is a simple exercise with a number of variations. The primary objective is to teach the dog to perform the teeter completely, without regard to the position taken by the handler.

Two variations of the exercise are used. In the first variation the dog performs the teeter in the direction of a target placed 12' to 15' away. The target should be baited, or it can be touched by the dog in anticipation of a deferred reward.

In the second variation, the dog performs the teeter in the direction of a table set 12' to 15' away. The table should be baited, or it can be touched by the dog in anticipation of a deferred reward.

In both variations the handler will assume a variety of positions in relationship to the dog while performing the teeter. These should include:

- Working at a lateral distance with the dog on right.

- Working at a lateral distance with the dog on left.

- Recalling the dog over the teeter.

- Sending the dog away over the teeter.

Playing Double Dog Dare Ya

You'll need a timekeeper, a scribe, and a judge to conduct the game. Enlist your students for these tasks.

Brief your students on the rules of the game. Remind them that it is only a game. It is more important that they attend to their own dogs' motivation, safety, and attitude than it is to win some silly training game.

The game begins and ends at the same line. Each dog and handler will have 55 seconds to accumulate as many points as possible. The dog *must* cross the finish line before time elapses. The timekeeper will blow a warning whistle at 50 seconds, and dogs must cross the line before the second whistle, or all points are reduced by half. Obstacles can be taken multiple times for points, but not back-to-back. Dropped bars will *not* be reset during the run. The weave poles are judged without faults. That is, there is no fault for an improper entry, or a missed pole, but the error must be corrected or no points are earned.

Obstacle values are:

- Jumps: 1 point;

- Tunnels and tire: 3 points;

- Weave poles and contact obstacles: 5 points.

The A-frame has no point value. However, when performed correctly, all points earned to that point are doubled. When performed incorrectly (missed contact), all points are halved. A dog and handler team can double points as often as they have time for, but must perform at least one obstacle correctly between each attempt to double.

The most points earned wins the game. In case of a tie, time decides the winner.

Use the equipment setup shown on the Facility Layout. Designate one side of the field as the start.

Go the Distance

Week 1: Student Notes

"Working your dog at a distance" is a misnomer. It gives the wrong impression of what is actually going on. This training plan is devoted, instead, to teaching you and your dog to work at a distance apart as a team.

The ability to work at a distance apart benefits the agility team in a variety of ways. In a Standard class you will find yourself able to send the dog ahead to perform long sequences, while taking the shorter, more direct route. This compels the dog to greater speed to keep up.

Nancy Krouse-Culley

More emphasis is placed on the desired performance of technical obstacles. So the dog performs more accurately, and also more reliably. Discrimination problems become routine to the team with a solid repertoire of skills for communicating the desired action.

Working a distance apart from your dog is not a gimmick or trick. While it is good preparation for USDAA and NADAC Gamblers classes, you cannot continue to run your dog in Standard classes as though you are attached by Velcro, and then suddenly, in some 12-second window, stop flat-footed and send your dog away to work without you. It doesn't work that way.

Distance is a working style, which must be constantly with you in competition, whether in Standard classes, Jumpers classes, or the games.

Don't confine your willingness to work at a distance apart from your dog to training. Take it with you into competition. Be willing to test your developing repertoire. Be bold. Train the way you compete; compete the way you train.

Fundamentals of *Left* and *Right* Directionals

The first step in teaching directional commands is to review your own skills at determining your left from right. When issuing a *Left* or *Right* command you will always be directing the dog to its left and right, *not* your own.

Keep it simple for your canine counterpart and only work one directional per session in the beginning. Switching from *Left* to *Right* without allowing time for either one to begin to sink in may be confusing and inhibit the learning process. You want to be very sure that the dog is assimilating the information you are providing and not just patterning a left movement, followed by a right movement, followed by a left, and so on.

By choosing either *Left* or *Right* to begin with, you can expect the dog to start processing the information by the conclusion of the first lesson. Keeping the sessions short and working a few times per day will allow you to work the alternate direction on the same day. But be sure to only ask for one directional per session. After the first day or so, when the dog begins to better understand each command, and you can combine the lefts and rights in each session.

1. Place the dog on a wait, in any position, on the side of choice—left for *Left* or right for *Right*.

2. Toss the favored toy away from your body using a lateral outward sweep with your arm. At the same time issue the *Right* or *Left* command. Make sure that when you release the toy that it does indeed go the intended direction and that your dog makes a definitive left or right turn. It is important that the directional command is given as the dog turns the appropriate direction to insure the word to behavior association.

3. Repeat this process several times, remembering that it is not only teaching a directional, but also helping to build a great attitude toward working with you.

The same process should be applied for the opposite directional. In the next session switch to the other side and repeat the exercise several more times.

Leash Work

You can immediately begin to supplement your *Left* and *Right* directionals training in many ways while interacting with your dog at home. When you're out for a walk with your dog, use your leash and a directional command, either *Left* or *Right*, to warn your dog of a change of direction.

1. While free heeling (allowing your dog to forge ahead), wait for a moment in which you are directly behind your dog as he walks or forges ahead. Initially don't allow the dog to move ahead any further than about 4'.

2. At random moments give your command to turn (either *Right* or *Left*).

3. Tug the leash in the desired direction and make your turn.

Don't be punitive. This isn't an exercise intended to inflict pain. What you're trying to do is give the dog warning that you are turning right or left. Eventually he will begin to recognize a pattern in your strange behavior, and anticipate the turn by *learning* the difference in your behavior based on whether you say *Right* or you say *Left*.

Once your dog begins to anticipate the turn based on your verbal command with less pressure from you tugging the lead, you can lengthen the lead so that the dog works at a greater distance from you.

Playing With Toys

You can supplement your teaching of *Left* and *Right* directionals while at play with your dog in the yard. No equipment other than a toy that can be thrown is required. *Left* and *Right* command training becomes a game to the dog and taps into his sense of fun.

Keep your expectations modest. Train with a sense of fun. Don't give harsh corrections; it won't seem very much like a game to your dog if you start getting serious about it.

1. Start with your dog at heel-side.

2. Walk forward with the toy in your left hand, teasing and enticing your dog with the toy.

3. Randomly, while you have your dog's rapt attention, throw the toy to the left. At that precise moment give your directional command *Left*.

4. Praise your dog lavishly for turning left to go after the toy.

5. Repeat this several times.

Your dog will learn the game quickly, turning rapidly to get the toy when he hears your *Left* command. When you see this anticipation, you will change the rules of the game just a bit. Start delaying the toss just a wee moment after giving the command. You want to see him turning left in *anticipation* of the toss, rather than just chasing after the toy as you toss it. Play with this subtly. You don't want to delay the toss so long that your dog is turning back toward you.

Teach the *Right* directional using the same steps.

As your dog begins to understand *Left* and *Right*, given the context above, you should use the same steps to have him turn across your body in response to the cue. For example, rather than tossing the toy left while the dog is on your left, toss the toy right while he is on your left. This is a more complex concept for the dog. It makes no matter where you are in relationship to him. *Left* is always left, and *Right* is always right.

Week 2: Instructor Notes

In the context of at-side working, the dog and handler might be a very comfortable and skilled working team. However, this new insistence by the handler to work at a distance will be as new to the dog as the first day he set foot on the teeter, and possibly just as disconcerting.

Cherie Gessford

You must monitor all of your students so that they are not too demanding of their dogs' progress. Think of it this way... for the entirety of his career the dog might only know the performance of the teeter or the weave poles in one context, that is, with the handler hovering directly over and micro-managing. If there is a distance between the dog and handler, it might be a signal to the dog that he has somehow done wrong. He'll be confused and disconcerted. To continue to drill a confused dog, insisting on maximum distance, might heighten the uncertainty and cause the dog to shut down.

You have to be on guard against this development.

Remind your students early on that they are teaching new skills to the dog. They should not have grand expectations right at the beginning. Distance work has to be graduated, much as you would slowly raise the jump heights for a novice dog.

Further, you'll have to ask your students to remember that in training a new concept they have to be completely enthusiastic in their praise and generous in their reward for small steps forward. Corrections should not be a part of the training program, or they should be entirely *neutral*.

Be prepared to add props to exercises to help a dog to succeed. For example, use a food treat as bait at the end of a contact obstacle to encourage the dog to work down through the contact, even when the handler is working at a distance. Point out to your students that *containment lines* are only guidelines, and that they should move in however much is necessary to ensure that the dog succeeds in an exercise.

Be compassionate, and be patient. Everything will work out.

Organizational Notes

Pass out this week's Student Notes. Take a poll. How many have started the *Left* and *Right* directionals training program? This is a good time to get on your soapbox and talk about the importance of the work-at-home exercises provided in the Student Notes. Some skills require a daily session with the dog and will not be learned during one night a week at the training center.

This week the Student Notes include an exercise for teaching a dog to *Get Out*. A lot of attention will be paid to the *Get Out* command over the course of this training program. It is a powerful directional, and necessary for the agility team that wishes to work a distance apart.

Discuss briefly with your class the difference between *Left* and *Right* directionals, and directionals like *Come* and *Get Out*. *Left* and *Right* directionals are absolute. That is, it is the dog's left and right without regard to the position of the handler. *Come* and *Get Out* are relative directionals. That is, the direction of the turn depends on (or is relative to) the handler's position.

Review the Instructor Notes about each dog's progress in the compulsory exercises from Week 1. It might be necessary to include exercises this week that will help strengthen foundation skills.

This is intended to be a two-hour class, conducted by two or more instructors. The instructors' responsibility is to keep things moving, maintain a balance, and see that everyone gets as much individual attention as possible.

How to Conduct the Class

Break this week's class into three periods as explained in the following sections.

WEEK 2

- **First Period: Free for All**—Allow everyone to work on whichever challenge they want. Because there are seven separate stations, a smaller number of instructors means that each must at times monitor more than one station to keep people focused and moving, and to help with handling dilemmas.

  Explain each of the distance challenges as though describing the parameters of the joker (or gamble) in a Gamblers class. But advise your students that it's more important that their dogs have a positive and successful experience than it is for them, the handlers, to honor an arbitrary containment line in order to look good in a training game.

- **Second Period: Demonstration**—By jump height, challenge one team at a time to do any *three* of the distance sequences (handler's choice!). Then conclude with jump and table. It's okay to do additional obstacles between sequences to establish flow. This is a good opportunity to discuss as a group what works, and what doesn't work, for each handler.

- **Third Period: Course Run**—Chain the sequences into a course. A suggested course sequence is shown in the Facility Layout. You can set any course that you like. However, the flow should reflect performance of the individual distance challenges illustrated in the training sets.

  Everybody should have a chance to walk this course. It might be worthwhile to mention to them prior to the walk-through that sequences they've practiced earlier in class might not be as neatly presented in the context of the course run. They'll have to make the effort to get their dogs lined up properly to have a fair chance at completing the distance challenges.

  Your students should *not* be required to maintain the containment lines.

  It's always a good idea when running a course in a training class to watch your students very closely. At the end of their complete run allow them to go back onto the course and work on problem areas. You can make handling suggestions that will help them through the difficult passages. You will find handling challenges on this course that weren't practiced during the working sets.

Week 2: Progress Worksheet

Instructors: **Date:**

Handler and Dog	Present	Notes

GENERAL NOTES:

Go the Distance

Week 2: Facility Layout

One square = 10'

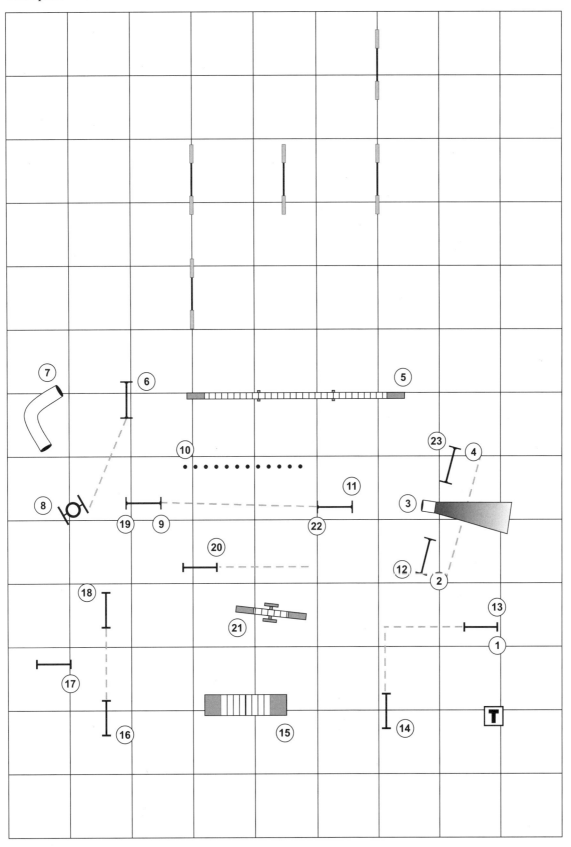

Week 2: Facility Layout Worksheet

Design your Facility Layout using a 1" = 10' scale (standard agility template)

Go the Distance

Week 2 Exercises: Get Out and Lateral Distance

The chief goal of this week's lesson plan is to give your students an opportunity for modest success. The lesson plan includes a variety of reasonable distance challenges, all of which your students can practice before putting them into use.

If you have enough room in your training center you may want to put up one or more of the exercises from Week 1 with which your students need more work.

Make sure that all of your instructors are familiar with all of the training sets in this lesson plan. It would be useful for them to work their own dogs on the drills, and have a go at the standard course run before the students have to do so. This is a valuable means of knowing what kinds of problems to expect.

Set 1: Get Out

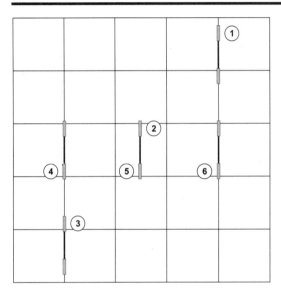

Before doing the *Get Out* exercise, you should reacquaint your students' dogs with approaches to depressed angle jumps. Green dogs may tend to refuse or run by a jump that isn't presented squarely. The following sequences are only reminders that sometimes the handler may ask the dog to perform a jump at a 45° angle, or perhaps something even more severe.

The first sequence is a simple loop that requires the dog to perform each of the first three jumps at a 45° angle. Make sure to line up the dog for the approach to jump #1 so that all three jumps are presented in a straight line.

The turn from jump #3 to #4 can be interesting. Instruct students to run with their dogs at the heel-side position. The turn will require either that the handler stays on the inside post position, or run out and cross in front to keep the dog on the handler's right for the line of jumps #4 through #6.

Do no more than one or two repetitions of this sequence.

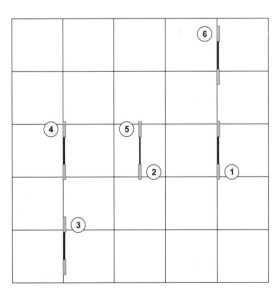

This sequence is far trickier than the first. The dog must be called off of, or pushed away from, the obvious next obstacle twice; once on the approach to #3, and again on the approach to #6.

Have your students devise their own plan of attack. There is no stipulation as to what handling technique(s) they should be using right now.

Do no more than one or two repetitions of this sequence.

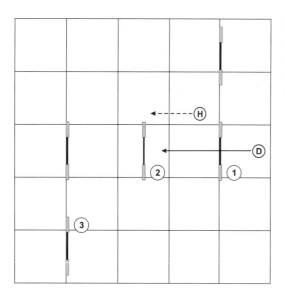

In this exercise the handler will take a modest lead-out from the dog. The length of the lead-out depends upon the speed of the dog and the quickness of the handler. It is imperative that the handler be able to intercept the dog on the landing side of the second jump of the sequence.

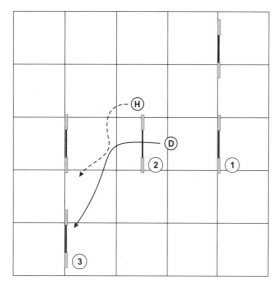

On the landing side of jump #2 the handler will *intrude* on the dog's path. This intrusion must be sudden, startling, and abrupt! The movement of the handler is virtually sideways in a perfectly timed step, which risks collision with the dog. Notice how the lines of handler and dog converge.

The idea is that the encroachment into the dog's path is so precipitous that after a suitable number of repetitions the dog will take the *Get Out* command as a warning to bounce away from the handler to engage the outside obstacle.

The sideways movement should include something of a *stomp* as the handler intrudes into the dog's space, a command to *Get Out*, and a hand signal pushing out to the #3 jump. All of the signals to the dog happen all at once. That is, sidestep, stomp, hand signal, and *Get Out* command are all pretty much simultaneous.

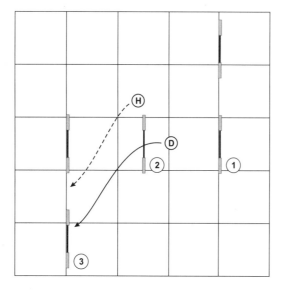

This illustration shows what you *don't* want to see happen. That is, the handler simply turns the corner on jump #2 and makes a beeline for jump #3. While the dog will follow this handling, it is doing nothing to teach the *Get Out* directional.

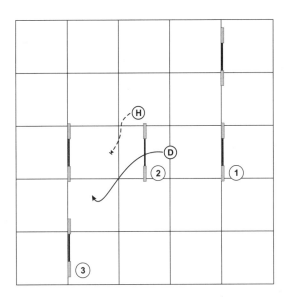

The illustration shows another handling flaw, the handler who wants to stop and point. The dog senses the handler's loss of motion and begins to curl back on the handler's position. This may result in a refusal, an off-course, or at the very least, lost time.

It's fundamental to this exercise that the handler really never stops moving. Avoid any kind of full stop while teaching *Get Out*.

WEEK 2

Set 2: Jump-Table

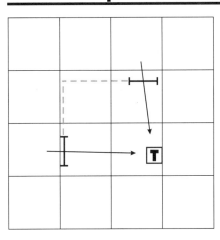

This is the fundamental distance challenge. The handler sends the dog over either jump, and onto the table.

Advise students to begin with a *happy table* exercise, if the dog won't instantly go away to the table Begin close to the table. Put bait on the table. Send the dog to the table to get the bait. Gradually back away, until the dog is performing the jump first to get to the table.

The directional command implicit in this exercise is *Go On* which means that the dog should keep going away from the handler. Follow the directional with the *Table* command.

Tell your students to allow their dogs to relax on the table. Sometimes you just want to let the dog go to the table happily rather than always compelling the dog to a specific performance.

Set 3: Jump-Teeter

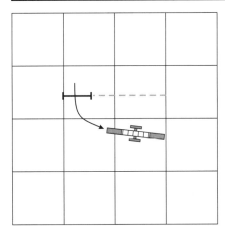

This exercise requires the dog to perform a complex obstacle at a modest distance from the handler. The handler should remain behind the containment line. Most handlers will be astonished to discover that their dogs will do this with little problem, and without them having to baby-sit the descent contact.

If the handler stops flat-footed as the dog is making the descent, it's likely that the dog will bail off sideways, and miss the contact. Advise your students to keep moving in a line parallel with the dog's path so that the dog will walk smartly off the end of the plank.

If the dog is sent to the opening jump squarely, the ascent to the teeter requires a change of direction. With the handler working down the containment line, a simple, well-timed *Come* should turn the dog to the teeter. However, if the approach to the jump has the dog's path pointed straight at the ascent to the teeter, it would be a mistake to tell the dog to *Come*, as the command would pull the dog off the teeter rather than help him get up on it.

If a dog is bailing off the teeter early, use a target to get the dog to drive straight off the teeter board.

Set 4: Jump 180

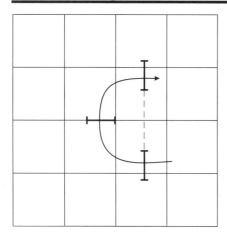

This is a very basic kind of send, but requires a directional command, *Go On*, and then *Jump*. The containment line that should be observed is drawn between the starting and ending jumps.

Remind your students that the *Go On* directional must be taught, as it is not intuitively known by their dogs. If the dog shows any hesitation, the handler should step in and direct the dog over the center jump. After several repetitions most dogs will understand the drill.

Make sure that handlers keep their dogs turning after the second jump. A simple *Come* will do. A turn of the handler's body, albeit at a distance, will assist the dog in the turn.

Set 5: Jump, Tunnel, Jump 180

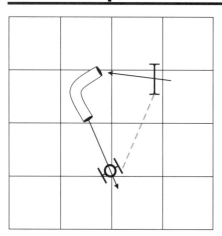

This is, of course, the classic novice gamble. Dogs should not learn this the hard way, in competition. They should have ample opportunity to give it a try in training class.

Surprisingly, a number of dogs will not automatically volunteer for the tunnel without the assistance of their handlers. Advise students having difficulty with this set to work the tunnel by itself for awhile, providing plenty of praise and treats for the dog on each successive repetition. Gradually send the dog to the tunnel from farther back, while hurrying to meet the dog coming out of the tunnel.

Add the jump, and add the tire when the dog is working away with great confidence.

Set 6: Jump Away, Back to the Tunnel

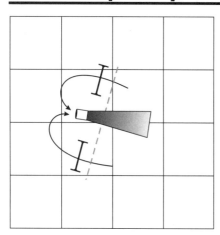

This exercise is a good test of a dog's understanding of the performance of the collapsed tunnel. Typically we present the tunnel to a dog as a gaping opening in a direct line. But here we are sending the dog out over a jump, expecting the performance of the tunnel without handler intervention. The containment line is just a pace from the opening jumps.

The handler can increase the dog's probability of success by moving in the direction the dog is required to turn after the jump. Use a *Come* command to help turn the dog smartly. A turn in the handler's body, almost away from the dog, should also help to turn the dog.

This exercise should be attempted from both sides.

Set 7: Jump and Weave Away

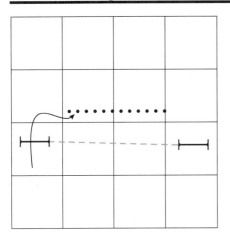

This set will amaze most handlers because they have no clue that their dogs will be able to weave without *handler assistance* (which can usually be defined as a hunkered over handler, with knees flapping, and hands flicking back and forth in front of the dog's face).

However, not all dogs will be able to do this exercise without faulting the poles. These handlers should be advised to do more work with the poles, helping their dogs to get the big picture with the aid of a clicker, or weave pole wires.

The set should be attempted in either direction so that one performance is on the heel-side, and the other on the off-side.

Again, there is a change of direction in this sequence. With the handler working down the containment line, use *Come* to turn the dog in the direction of the poles. This has to be well timed so that the dog lines up with the poles, and does not run out around them.

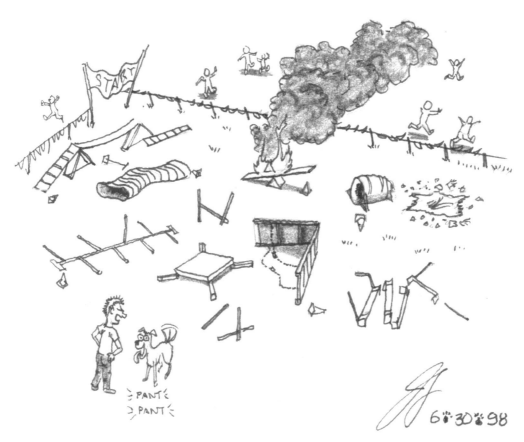

Jim Liddle

Okay, Mr. Excitement...Do you have an encore planned, or can we just crawl away in shame now?

Go the Distance

Week 2: Student Notes

The reason most dogs do not learn to work at a distance is that the trainers do not have a committed program to train the dogs to do so. Distance training, like simple sequence training, takes a vision of where you are going, a plan to get there, and a commitment to actually do the training. The vast majority of agility dogs do not know directionals, beyond *Come*, simply because their trainers have never made the attempt.

Bob Ebdon

Like training the weave poles, you should not expect to turn your dog into a gambling fool by relying on a once a week, one-hour romp on a training field. You must do some homework.

The training session from Week 2 included a modest inventory of distance challenges, providing a pretty good test of what your dog might be ready for. You might have been surprised by what your dog will do for you, as you maintain a modest distance.

At the same time, your instructors probably gave you tips about what you can do as a handler to increase the likelihood of success in distance work. Here are some additional tips:

- Don't leave your dog hanging out in space. At the first sign of confusion you should step in and give the dog direction.

- Standing flat-footed, pointing and shouting an obstacle command is usually not very good direction to the dog. Once you catch yourself flat-footed, and the dog is clearly confused, you need to step in immediately and show the dog the way.

- Try to establish flow into a sequence so that you and your dog are working at a smooth, brisk pace. At the same time take care to create a line in the dog's path that leads the dog through the sequence in his natural stride.

- Use your body for directional cues. Turn, face, and move in the direction of the flow.

- Any time a change of direction is required, you should have a command for the change of direction. Don't rely solely on the name of the next obstacle to turn the dog.

Working the Dog Left and Right

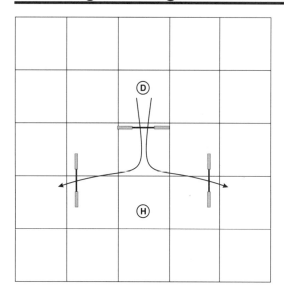

For this exercise you'll call upon your skills in determining left or right based on your dog's position. Remember that *Left* and *Right* in the context we are using them dictate that a dog go a certain direction based on one verbal cue and the other direction based on a separate verbal cue. It makes no matter what direction you, the handler, are facing. It is not *your* left and right, it is *the dog's* left and right.

1. Position the dog in front of the first jump.

2. Lead out 12' or so beyond jump #1. Turn and face the dog. Call the dog toward you over the jump.

3. As the dog commits to the jump, begin your turn and give the *Left* or *Right* command. Be careful that your command is not too early. This could easily cause the dog to drop a leg as he negotiates the change of direction and take down a rail.

Have the dog's toy ready. His learning will be well served in this exercise by an instant reward.

Do several repetitions of each direction. Let the dog be the indicator of how many times to repeat the exercise.

Asking the dog to perform the *Left* and *Right* directionals while you are facing him should not be a problem as long as the you use the correct cue.

Leading Out

There are two instances in a Standard class where you might choose to lead out from your dog: at the starting line and while the dog is on the table. In the latter case, you typically have about five seconds to get into the desired position.

We have all observed in competition handlers who *attempt* to lead out, but find their dogs breaking from the stay at the line. Sometimes this is a minor annoyance. If the dog breaks before the timekeeper is ready, the handler can saunter back to the line and reset the dog. However, if the timer's watch is on the line, the consequences of the dog breaking the stay can sometimes be disastrous. The dog might run past the first jump, causing the handler to return to the start of the course and redirect the dog. In the AKC this is faulted as a refusal. In any case, the dog moving will cost the team valuable time.

The purpose of the following exercise to develop a confident lead-out for you agility repertoire. You should do this kind of exercise frequently. Remember that the Rule of 5000 applies—anything you do 5000 times, you own.

The Stay
Face it, this part of the exercise is obedience. You should start your stay training on the flat, away from agility obstacles. But even when you start inserting obstacles between yourself and the dog, you will observe these steps:

1. Put your dog in a sit, stand, or down position.

2. Give a *Stay* command.

3. Turn, and walk away to your calling point.

4. If the dog breaks the stay, quietly return to the dog and physically *place* him back in the spot you left him. *Do not say Stay again.* Return to your calling point.

5. Call your dog to you; praise, and reward.

The most important part of this system is that you follow the system. Do it the same way, every time, without fail. The first time you give your dog permission to break a stay, without giving a correction, you have undone yourself. This is tedious and boring, and absolutely necessary.

The moment you introduce a jump between yourself and the dog, you have changed the exercise. You may find a dog that was previously doing magnificent stays and recalls for you suddenly will insist on breaking the stay. Don't panic, and don't give up. Just follow the system very calmly and very persistently.

If you go into competition before you have proofed your dog's stay you had better not lead out. In competition most judges won't allow you to train in the ring. Again, if you give your dog permission to break a stay by not giving a correction, you've undone your work on this skill.

The Call Over

When training a stay for agility purposes it is a good idea to introduce a jump in front of the dog early on. This is because 99% of all courses will begin with a jump. You want the dog to understand that the reward for staying will be a release over the jump. When a dog breaks the start, he is doing so to get to the obstacles as soon as possible. Why not build on this to get those rock solid stays you are looking for?

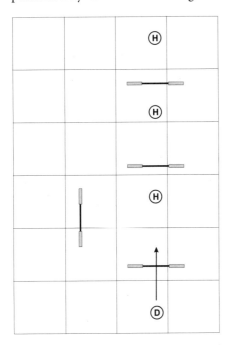

Start by leaving your dog in a stay and recalling him over a single jump. When the dog has maintained the stay position for a moment, release over the jump and praise, praise, praise!

If the dog breaks, replace the dog behind the jump and try again. Remember that you are *always* working on developing a reliable stay. The steps described in the previous section must still be religiously observed.

Remind your dog that you are doing an obedience exercise by combining other obedience elements. Do a few brief heeling patterns before starting the jumping sequences. Then, as you work on the stay, you should alternately sit-stay, stand-stay, and down-stay your dog at the start line.

The goal is to teach the dog that the quicker he complies with your direction, the sooner you will release him over the obstacle. You use the jump as a reward instead of walking in and feeding the dog.

It's time to start thinking about what *your* job is, as the handler. Don't think of your dog as a wind-up toy that will perform at the push of a button. You have a substantial responsibility to give multiple unambiguous signals to direct your dog.

When calling your dog to you over a jump, don't just say *Jump* and stand there like a lump. Bend over, point your arm down at the center of the jump, establish eye contact with your dog, and say *Come, Jump*. Immediately praise your dog, give him a treat, and celebrate his performance.

When you've had several solid repetitions using one jump, include a second jump in the exercise. Again, use your body and point, giving the commands to *Come, Jump*. Make sure that you are clearly framed to your dog in the center of the two jumps.

Be prepared now for a new correction. If your dog runs around the first jump (a refusal), tell him *Wrong*, or some other operative word, and place him back behind the first jump. Don't praise him and don't give him a treat. But don't be angry either. Be neutral. Back up to a single jump recall. When you've done this successfully, then try the two-jump recall again.

When you are getting very reliable performances in a two-jump recall, you can begin doing a three-jump recall. The same rules apply as described for a two-jump recall.

The Turn

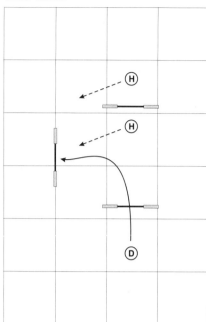

Occasionally a recall might require something more complex than a straight-over recall. A turn, for instance, might be needed.

Set up a simple 90° turn. Recall your dog over the single bar, then immediately turn the dog left (or right).

When doing a turn from a call-ahead position, you must communicate the turn using body movement. Notice that the handling path in the illustration is lateral toward the jump, but also forward, toward the dog.

After several successful repetitions, move your calling position back behind the second jump and do the same maneuver.

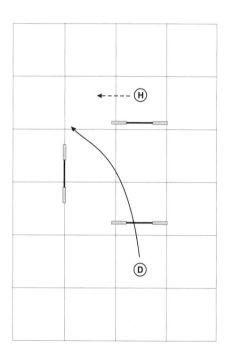

If *your* movement is not adequate to communicate the turn to your dog, he will move past the jump after the turn as though he did not see it.

You really can't correct your dog for this, because it wasn't his fault. It was yours. Your dog will respect you if every now and then you admit *my fault!* Be sure that your movement is dramatic.

You might find yourself struggling with the timing. If your dog takes off like a shot you will have to really scoot. Give an *early* command. Point your arm dramatically. Command your dog to *Go Left, Jump*.

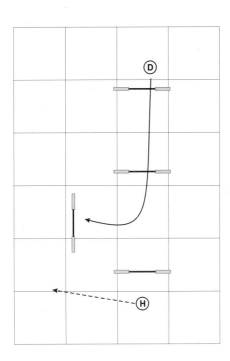

When you and your dog are doing a pretty reliable jump-then turn, try a two-jump-then-turn sequence.

Your timing will need to be pretty sharp in this exercise. You have to stay in position until the dog is committed to the second jump. If you move early you could cause him to run out around the second jump by your movement. So you have to wait until just the right moment, then move, point, and give the command.

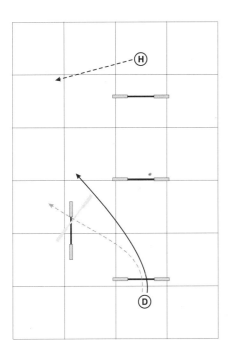

This is considerably more difficult than anything you've yet done. You will attempt to turn the dog after one jump, when you have put three jumps between you and your dog. You'll find the dog *much* more likely to run out past the jump after the turn. If this happens, you may want to rotate the jump so that it is presented at more of a 45° angle to the dog as shown in the illustration.

This is a difficult exercise. Most handlers can hardly move fast enough or dramatically enough to communicate the change of direction to the dog.

Week 3: Instructor Notes

The ability to work a dog at a distance is an extension of the ability to work the dog at side. The movement of the handler's body, the use of forward motion, turns, lead-hand cues, and verbal cues work on the same principles of doggie dynamics, whether the dog is working 4' away from the handler or 20'.

Nancy Krouse-Culley

The ingredients in the recipe for distance work that transform the dog working close with comfort and reliability to one that works at a distance with comfort and reliability, are experience and confidence. It is the obligation of the dog's trainer to begin the work with handling a modest distance away from the dog, and over time to stretch that distance.

Like all agility work this training cannot be rushed. Distance is added only gradually, and never faster than the dog is prepared to work.

The lesson plans contained in this workbook present a specific training foundation with the ultimate goal to enhance the ability of the dog and handler to work at a distance apart. The basic training is comprised of several skill areas, each requiring attention and commitment to training from your students. The skill areas include: directionals, obstacle discrimination, technical obstacle performance at a distance, sending a dog away to perform an obstacle or obstacles, and other skills.

It's your obligation, as an agility instructor to present the training concepts and help your students visualize the training goals. In this respect you are a facilitator. You aren't training your students' dogs. That's their job.

An individual exercise is not an *end game*. It is a means by which you show your students *how* a skill is trained. It allows you to work on matters of timing and handling with them, so that they can go back to their own training programs and apply what they've learned.

Organizational Notes

This week's lesson plan makes use of a number of containment lines, which define a minimum distance the handler should be from her dog in order to score points in the practice competition.

The class is taught in the context of a game. That means that the competitive juices will be flowing and your students will abandon thoughts of doing what's right for their dogs for the sake of doing well and looking good. Therefore, the game provides a useful context for testing the dog's understanding of the lessons of the day while the handler is in the more frantic mode of competition.

Remind them early to forget about the game. They have to show an awareness of the distance away their dogs are willing to work, and what obstacles their dogs will perform at that distance. It is more important to attend to their dogs' training than to do well in a silly training game.

Here are some basic guidelines so that your students will not allow their dogs to fail:

- *Containment lines* are only guidelines in training. The handler moves in as close to the action as necessary so that the action doesn't come to a stop.

- Pass up on difficult sequences that a dog is not prepared to understand.

- Remind handlers to praise and reward their dogs for even minor accomplishments.

How is everyone doing with homework? Ask if anyone wants to give a demonstration of something her dog has learned at home.

How to Conduct the Class

This class is conducted in a unique format. You'll teach your students a Gamblers game. But this is not the classic Gamblers. The game is called Timed Gamblers—Freestyle. Aside from incorporating some very specific distance challenges, this game will also introduce your student to the concept of timing, and the elements of point-accumulation strategy.

In a two-hour breakdown format this class would be conducted in this fashion:

- **First Period: Game**—Your students will play the game as described in "Playing the Game: Timed Gamblers—Freestyle".

  Make sure to allow enough time to give all of your students an opportunity to run. Because the game is played in fixed time periods, this is easy to calculate.

- **Second Period: Practice Sets**—You will break down the class into groups and practice the various *joker* challenges as described in "The Joker Training Sets".

- **Third Period: Repeat Game**—Your students will play the game a second time, hopefully with greater success than their first outing.

  In a one-hour format, you probably won't have time for a playing the game twice. It's probably more important to do the working sets than to play the game.

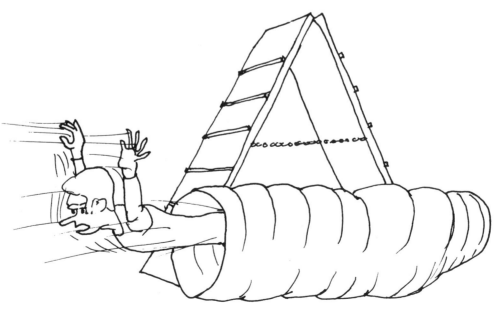

The block...

Roger Brucker

Go the Distance

Week 3: Progress Worksheet

Instructors: **Date:**

Handler and Dog	Present	Notes

GENERAL NOTES:

Week 3: Facility Layout

One square = 10'

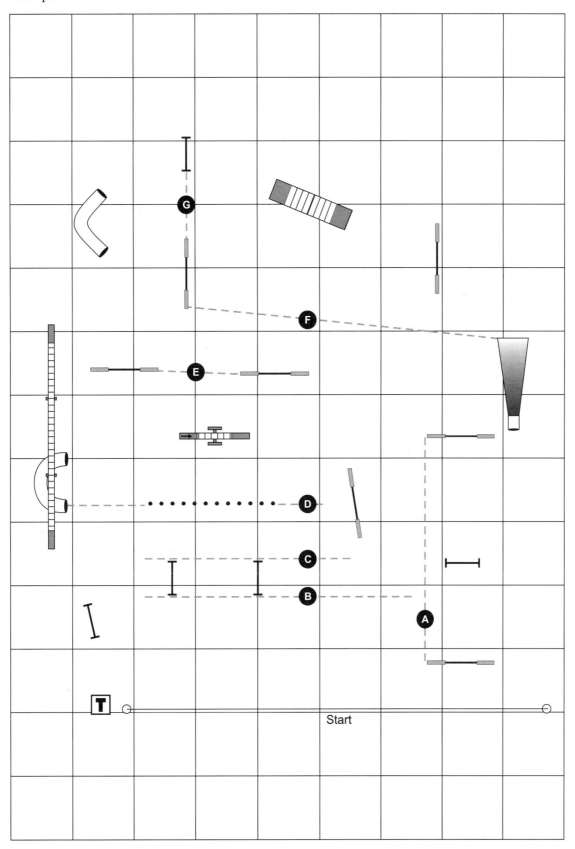

Start

T

Week 3: Facility Layout Worksheet

Design your Facility Layout using a 1" = 10' scale (standard agility template)

Week 3 Exercises: More Get Out Work

The goal of this week's lesson plan is to give your students some solid work training the *Get Out* command on modest distance challenges, providing them with ample opportunity for success. Because the class is delivered in the context of a game, you should have a watchful eye to ensure that your students are attending to the motivation of their dogs and are not getting caught up in the competition itself.

The homework from the Week 2 Student Notes included a *Get Out* training exercise. Who did the homework? You might want to remind your students that the homework exercises supplement the training they get in class, and enhance their dogs' chances of success.

You should explain to your students that the exercises here are intended to associate a performance or behavior with the command you are giving to that behavior, in this case, *Get Out*. It is important for the dog to do the performance, more so than it is for the handler to honor an arbitrary containment line. The student should be intent on watching for the dog's head to turn the appropriate direction. It is the head that steers the dog. If your students are watching that explicit body part, the exercises will go easier.

The Joker Training Sets

Note that this lesson plan represents a significant compression of training steps for each of the working sets or stations. Instructors should be prepared to repeat steps, or make expectations for the exercises more modest in nature in order that the dogs may succeed and learn at their own pace.

In any distance send-away, should the dog fail to understand the cue to *Get Out*, then the student should be instructed to step in and show the dog the way.

Set 1

In this set you are introducing the dogs to the *Get Out* command. *Get Out* is the reciprocal command to *Come*. *Come* tells the dog to bend his path in toward the handler; *Get Out* tells the dog to bend his path away from the handler.

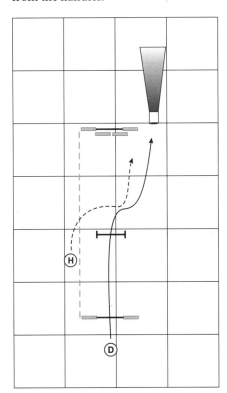

In the first approach, handlers should ignore the containment line. Also, block the dummy jump alongside the collapsed tunnel with extra jump wings so that the dog is not enticed by it.

Handlers should begin with a modest lead-out on the handler side of the containment line. As the dog lands over the second jump, the handler comes across aggressively, gives an off-arm signal, and tells the dog to *Get Out*. All of these actions occur in the same instant.

An off-arm signal is one given with the arm and hand opposite the side the dog is working. In this sequence, the handler will use the left arm to signal. It has the effect of communicating a change of direction to the dog.

Have your students do at least two repetitions of this approach. The dogs should be readily turning and seeking out the entry to the tunnel on the handler's *Get Out* command.

Repeat the exercise, taking one of the blocking wings away from the dummy jump. Have your students do at least two repetitions of this exercise. The dogs should be readily turning and seeking out the entry to the tunnel on the handler's *Get Out* command. If the dog actually jumps the narrow opening left at the jump, simplify the exercise by blocking the entire span of the dummy jump again.

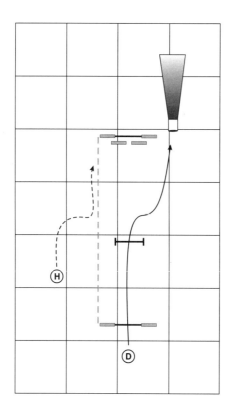

Next, have your students begin honoring the containment line. Note, however, that the handler starts at a lateral distance from her dog. This allows her to *sell* to the dog the notion that she is encroaching on his path, so that the dog will scoot out of the way and make the entry to the collapsed tunnel.

Again, use extra jump wings to block access to the dummy jump since you have added the complexity of having the handler honor the containment line.

Have your students do at least two repetitions of this approach. The dogs should be readily turning and seeking out the entry to the tunnel on the handler's *Get Out* command.

Next, repeat the exercise, taking one of the blocking wings away from the dummy jump, and work for the *Get Out* from the proper side of the containment line.

Have your students do at least two repetitions of this exercise. The dogs should be readily turning and seeking out the entry to the tunnel on the handler's *Get Out* command. If the dog jumps the narrow opening left at the jump, simplify the exercise by blocking the entire span of the jump, and also having the handler again encroach onto the dog's path.

Set 2

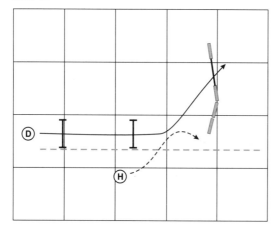

Here you will continue work on the *Get Out* command.

Notice that two extra jump wings are being used to block the dog's escape path. This makes the wing jump the most logical place for him to move. Again, the handler is going to initially ignore the containment line.

Handlers should begin with a modest lead-out on the handler side of the containment line. As the dog lands over the second jump, the handler comes across aggressively, gives an off-arm signal, and tells the dog to *Get Out*. All of these actions occur in the same instant.

Have your students do at least two repetitions of this approach. The dogs should be readily turning and seeking out the wing jump on the handler's *Get Out* command.

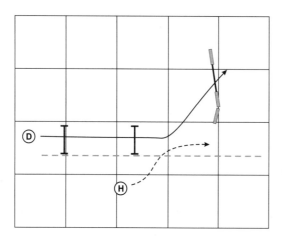

Next, remove one of the blocking wings (the one closest to the containment line), and repeat the exercise. However, this time the handler begins at more lateral distance in order to sell the idea of encroachment to the dog, and doesn't intrude quite so much onto the dog's path.

Have your students do at least two repetitions of this approach. The dogs should be readily turning and seeking out the bar of the jump on the handler's *Get Out* command. If a dog tends to pull back toward the handler, this is where you will see it. The handler's extra step inside the containment line will help sell the *Get Out*.

Go the Distance

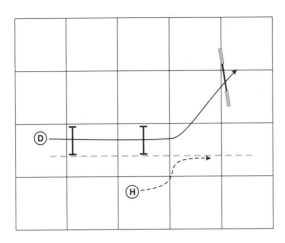

The third approach is pretty much the end-game in this exercise. The handler starts at yet a bit more lateral distance from the dog's path, and will honor the containment line.

Remind your students that they really have to sell the encroachment to the dog, even though they won't actually encroach on the dog.

Have your students do at least two repetitions of this approach. The dogs should be readily turning and seeking out the bar of the jump on the handler's *Get Out*. If the dog pulls back toward the handler, you'll have to simplify the exercise either by adding a blocking wing, getting the handler to step inside the containment line, or both.

Set 3

This set is very similar to Set 2 in its progression. Your students should work with Set 2 before working on this set, as it builds on the work done in the previous set. The only real difference is that this set does not use wings, as fences, to help direct the dog's path.

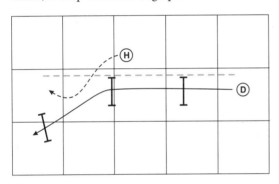

In the first approach, ignore the containment line.

Handlers should begin with a modest lead-out on the handler side of the containment line. As the dog lands over the second jump, the handler comes across aggressively, gives an off-arm signal, and tells the dog to *Get Out*. All of these actions occur in the same instant.

Have your students do at least two repetitions of this approach. The dogs should be readily turning and seeking out the bar of the jump on the handler's *Get Out* command. If a dog tends to pull back toward the handler, this is the approach where you will see it. The handler's extra step inside the containment line will help sell the *Get Out*.

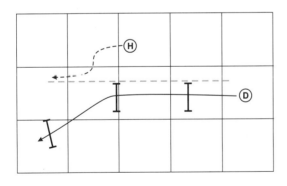

In the second approach, the handler starts with more lateral distance from the dog's path, and honors the containment line. Remind your students that they really have to sell the encroachment to the dog, even though the handler won't actually encroach on the dog.

Have your students do at least two repetitions of this approach. The dogs should be readily turning and seeking out the bar of the jump on the handler's *Get Out* command. If the dog pulls back toward the handler, simplify the exercise by getting the handler to step inside the containment line.

Set 4

This set continues work on the *Get Out* command. This time a technical obstacle at a modest distance is incorporated into the dog's performance. The weave poles serve as a portion of the containment line. A target is included at the end of the teeter. The target should be loaded with a good treat to keep the dog working in a straight line off the ramp. It should be placed close enough to the bottom of the ramp that the dog will hold the contact.

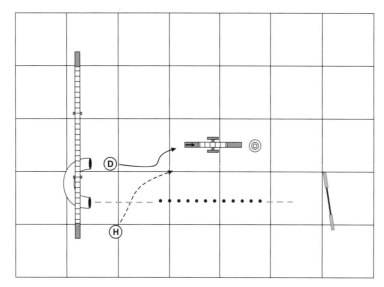

In the first approach the handler will not honor the containment line. The dog will first perform the weave poles, and then go into the tunnel. The handler should hang back a bit. As the dog comes out of the tunnel the handler encroaches to push the dog up to the teeter. The handler should give the *Get Out* command only if the dog initially turns back toward her. Otherwise, the teeter is presented in a straight line from the tunnel and a *Get Out* command might be inappropriate because you want the dog to maintain the straight line, and not bend away.

Do at least two repetitions.

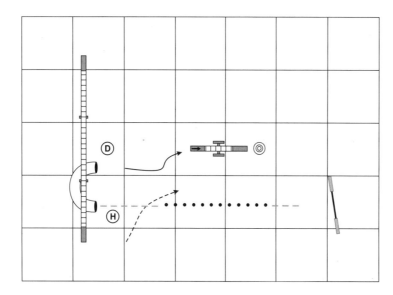

In the second approach, the handler should encroach less intrusively. That is the only real difference in the exercise. However, the handler still should not honor the containment line.

Do at least two repetitions of this approach.

The dog should remember the target and happily go on to the performance of the teeter.

Go the Distance

WEEK 3

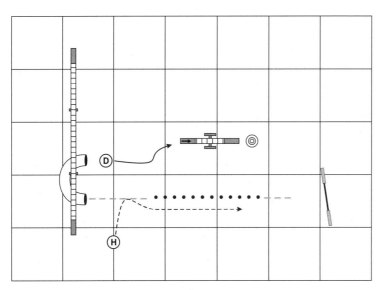

In the final approach, the handler will run up toward the containment line (but no further) to sell the dog on the idea of encroachment, and give a good *Get Out* command. The handler will then remain behind the containment line and work parallel with the dog.

Note that if the handler is too close to the line when getting the dog into the tunnel, she'll need to move away from the line while the dog is in the tunnel. This will give the handler room to move back in toward the line so that the dog knows what direction to move when exiting the tunnel.

Do at least two repetitions of this approach. If the dog pulls in to the handler's position, the exercise should be simplified by the handler again encroaching on the dog's path to sell the *Get Out*.

Set 5

This set features a pinwheel jump arrangement. It continues work on the *Get Out* command with a bit of a twist. The intention is to teach the dog to veer away from the handler's intended path, even though the handler might be behind the dog's position. In this case, the cross is supplemented by a broad lead-hand change, and the handler crossing behind the dog's position.

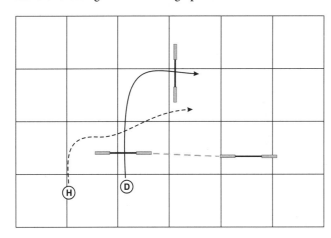

In the first repetition, the handler crosses *aggressively* behind the dog on the landing side of the first jump, changes lead-hands in a broad off-arm move, and steps over the dog's path, while giving the *Get Out* command. All of this happens as the same instant. The handler will not honor the containment line in this repetition.

This approach might have to be repeated several times, until the dog is moving naturally away from his handler.

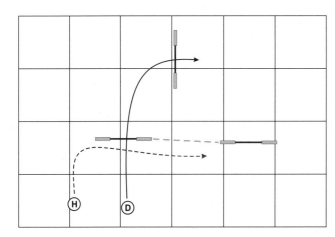

In the second approach, the handler crosses on the take-off side of the first jump. All other elements of the exercise are the same.

Do several repetitions of this approach.

If the dog tucks inside of the second jump, start the exercise again.

Set 6

This set continues work on the *Get Out* command used with a technical obstacle. A target is included at the end of the A-frame. The target should be loaded with a good treat to keep the dog working in a straight line off the ramp. It should be placed close enough to the bottom of the ramp that the dog will hold the contact.

You may want to simplify this exercise by moving the left end of the containment line from the bottom of the jump, to the top of the jump. Refer to the illustration to understand how to reposition the containment line.

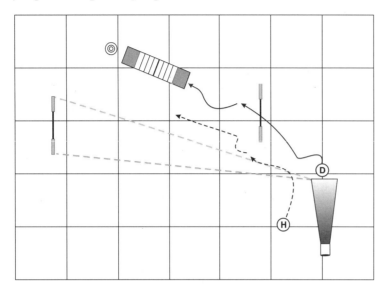

In the first approach, the handler will not honor the containment line. The dog will first perform the collapsed tunnel. The handler should hang back a bit, so that as the dog comes out of the tunnel, the handler can step forward to push the dog to the jump. Give a *Get Out* command to push the dog to the jump if the dog turns back toward the handler after the tunnel.

A *Get Out* might also be required before the A-frame, if the dog turns back to the handler after the jump. Notice that the handler should conserve a bit of room to step in toward the dog in case the *Get Out* is needed.

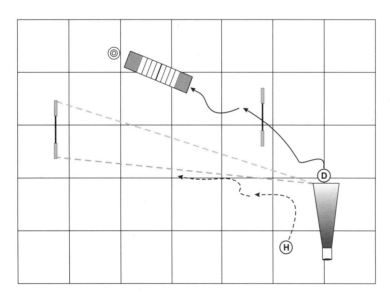

In the final approach to the exercise, the handler stays behind the containment line. The handler should reserve enough distance from the containment line to have room to push forward to convince the dog of the correct direction to travel at the same time the *Get Out* command is given.

If the dog turns back toward the handler after the jump, she may have to give a *Get Out* command to push the dog out to the A-frame.

Set 7

This set has nothing to do with the *Get Out* command. Everyone can use a break. This is the classic novice gamble, which is taught by use of modest backchaining and a target at the end of the sequence. The target should be loaded with a good treat to keep the dog motivated.

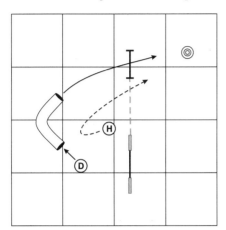

The dog starts through the tunnel and goes over the nonwinged jump, where he is allowed to collect the treat at the target.

The handler does not honor the containment line in this approach. However, when the dog gets in the tunnel, the handler pushes to get on the opposite side of the final jump to be in position to call the dog over and to show the treat.

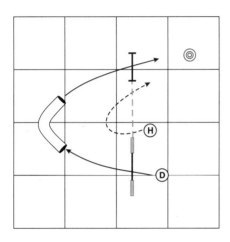

In the second approach, the dog starts over the first jump, is directed through the tunnel, and goes over the nonwinged jump, where he is allowed to collect the treat at the target.

Again, the handler does not honor the containment line. However, when the dog gets in the tunnel, the handler pushes to get on the opposite side of the final jump to be in position to call the dog over and to show the treat.

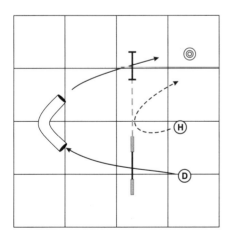

In the final approach, the handler will honor the containment line.

Remind your students to give a good running start at the first jump so that they are not standing still at any time during the performance of this distance challenge.

Playing the Game: Timed Gamblers—Freestyle

Timed Gamblers—Freestyle is an important variation of Timed Gamblers. It is important because this variation is quickly becoming the favored form of the game since it provides much richer opportunities for strategy and cunning. The game still retains the demands for a handler to have a good understanding of the speed at which his dog works. This version of Timed Gamblers is often used as a team game in the USDAA's Dog Agility Masters (DAM) Team tournaments.

Briefing

The purpose of this game is for the handler to accumulate the maximum number of points in the time allowed.

The game is divided into two periods of fixed time: 40 seconds and 15 seconds. In the first period the dog earns points for each obstacle performed successfully. Any obstacle can be performed only twice for points.

The timekeeper will blow a whistle indicating the end of the 40-second period.

In the second period all point values are doubled. Any points earned by the dog can be kept *only* if the dog finishes before the overall time expires. All doubled points are lost if the dog does not finish in time.

The number of times an obstacle was performed in the first period is wiped clean for the double-point period. Again, the dog will be allowed to perform any given obstacle only twice for the doubled points.

If a dog is in the midst of an obstacle performance when the whistle blows ending the first point-accumulation period, the points are doubled for that obstacle.

For the purposes of this class only, include the following modification to the rules of the game. This course has a number of *jokers*, or distance challenges, for point accumulation. If the handler stays behind the indicated line for the joker, then points for that performance are doubled in the 40-second point accumulation periods and doubled twice in the second period.

Scoring

Timed Gamblers—Freestyle is scored points, then time. The greatest number of points wins. Time is used as a tie-breaker only.

Point Values of Obstacles

Obstacle	Opening Period	Bonus Period
Jumps	1 point	2 points
Tunnels and tire	3 points	6 points
Contacts and weave poles	5 points	10 points

The scribe will record points earned by a dog in two separate columns, one representing the regular score for an obstacle performance, and one representing a score to be doubled by the scorekeeper. All points in the doubled column will be lost if the total time is higher than the time set by the judge.

Use the course shown in the Facility Layout, or design your own Timed Gamblers—Freestyle course.

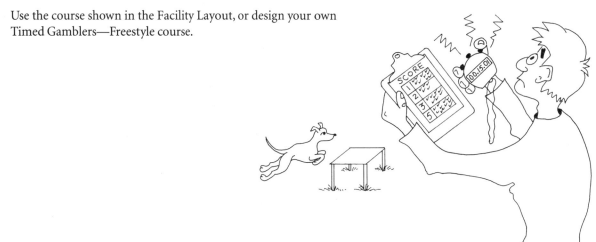

Go the Distance

Week 3: Student Notes

One of the primary keys to properly training a dog for agility, whether for simple at side work, or for working at a distance, is to cultivate and maintain the sense of fun for the dog. This is an issue of motivation.

A reluctant or worried dog may be compelled to work at his handler's side. But the work will be lackluster, without the speed or motivation desirable for a top performance. Ask the reluctant or worried dog to work at a distance and... well, forget it. You will not get distance work out of this dog.

So what is the magic element that makes or breaks the dog's sense of fun and his motivation for the sport of agility?

In a nutshell, it is the value association with the sport, either positive or negative.

Valerie Pietraszewska

Negative associations are inspired and reinforced by the dog's trainer. That would be you. If you treat the dog harshly, inflict some sort of pain, or beat up the dog emotionally, he will not consider agility very fun at all.

When we use words and phrases like "treating the dog harshly", "inflicting pain", "beating up the dog", it seems clear cut what kind of actions we should avoid. But the dog is a sensitive creature. Sometimes negative associations can be very subtle. In this subtlety a trainer often will not realize what he or she is doing and will unwittingly do damage to the dog's association with agility that will be difficult to fix.

Start by endeavoring to never say *No* to your dog as a correction. In the first place, many performance errors are errors by the handler. It is certainly inappropriate to blame the dog for a handler's error. Also, the word *No* is only an obvious negative. There are many sounds you can make that are clearly negatives.

Corrections should always be neutral. Reward should be positive and, where appropriate, enthusiastic. If you use a balanced system of correction and reward, the dog will figure out in a hurry what pleases you and will become a better agility dog.

Get Outs Without Agility Equipment

The beauty of teaching the *Get Out* command is that it allows you, the handler, to not only shorten the distance you must travel to direct your dog around the course, but also enables you to excel in other areas of competition, namely, Gamblers classes.

Get Out is a directional command that is an aid both on the flat and during the actual negotiation of the obstacles. It is one of the most important directional tools you can teach your dog. Also, it can be taught amazingly fast with little extra effort at home or when actual obstacles are not available.

Your homework assignment is to spend the week teaching your dog to *Get Out* laterally around various stationary obstacles such as trees, garbage cans, chairs, lawn furniture. The list goes on and on. This week's class dealt exclusively with pushing your dog out to, over, and through obstacles. At home you can maximize its effectiveness by helping the dog understand the basic concept of moving away from you for a reward.

Start by getting your dog's favorite toy or treat and position the dog in a stay (sit, down, or stand) next to a stationary object. With the hand closest to the dog, signal a *Get Out* (that is, a sweeping sideways motion) while simultaneously using the verbal command. With the reward in the other hand, extend this arm toward the object that the dog is to *Get Out* around and toss the toy or give the treat as the dog moves off your side and goes around the object. Be sure to go both directions off both sides to avoid the *sidedness* issue once again. Once the dog catches on to the game, you can begin to ask the dog to go around bigger objects and to go farther away.

Another simple at-home *Get Out* exercise uses only you, the dog, and a favorite toy. Position the dog on your left or right side in a sit while holding the toy in the hand closest to the dog. Throw the toy laterally away from you as you command *Get Out*. Again, be sure to work off both your left and right side.

Increasing Distance With Directionals

This week will further the use of the two-jump sequence and begin to require the dog to go on ahead of you over jump #1. Offer a verbal directional cue as well as a physical cue from behind the dog to direct him over jump #2. Targeting the dog over jump #2 would be advised for the first few attempts.

Use targets the first time or two and then switch to tossing the toy or food tube. The target is a lure to help the dog understand the exercise. Once the dog understands the desired behavior, encourage thinking and problem solving on his part. The toy or food tube becomes the reward for choosing the correct behavior.

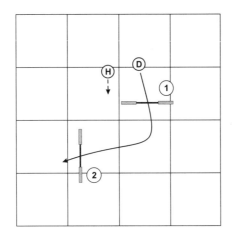

Place the dog in front of jump #1. Do not lead out. Send the dog over jump #1, as the dog commits to the jump begin your turn and issue the verbal directional cue followed by the command for jump #2.

If the dog hesitates to take even the first jump you should resort to targeting the dog for this obstacle, praising profusely the successful attempt. Once the dog is confidently going over the first jump, replace the target over jump #2.

The timing of your commands is crucial to your dog's success as well as to the dog's eventual understanding of the *Left* and *Right* commands. After initially showing the dog the way using the target, replace your target or lure with the instant reward of a toy being tossed over the jump as understanding begins to replace patterning.

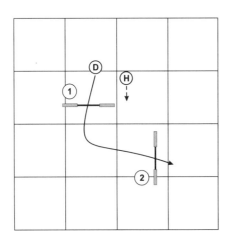

This exercise may be repeated five or six times in each direction. By this time you should be able to mix and match your *Left* and *Right* commands in each training session.

Take note of which direction your dog seems to be more comfortable with and be sure to ask for a ratio of two to one in favor of the less preferred side. Dogs, like people, are generally sided. This means they will be more likely to turn one direction over the other. This is perfectly normal and is easily rectified by increasing the number of repetitions to the side less used. Not all dogs are sided but, to a certain degree, the majority are. It will affect your dog's responsiveness to that particular direction if left unchecked. Be careful not to change your dog's preference, as opposed to correcting it, by eliminating the use of the directional to the preferred side altogether.

Week 4: Instructor Notes

This lesson plan is designed to evaluate the obstacle discrimination abilities of the dogs in your class. It is also going to give insight as to whether or not the obstacles have been properly taught. The ultimate goal of this week's lesson plan is to enhance the distance capabilities of your students by way of proper obstacle negotiation and awareness.

Very often the actual performance of an obstacle is overlooked in the whole distance scenario. How many times have your students specifically asked to work on *distance* this week? These are usually the same people that tend to baby-sit their dogs over, through, and across each obstacle as it is performed. The first step to any dog's distance capabilities is the understanding of proper obstacle negotiation *without* handler assistance. This means not allowing handlers to "become one with the obstacles".

Karen Gaydos

When instructing students how to teach each specific piece of equipment, you must caution them to begin to distance themselves from the obstacles as soon as possible. As the dog becomes confident on the equipment, lateral distance on the part of the handler should begin to be evident to the dog as he performs the obstacle. It should be each handler's goal that the dog sees each piece of equipment as a separate entity that she directs him to. When a command is given for a specific obstacle, the dog should essentially break away from the handler, turn his attention to the obstacle, perform that obstacle, and return his attention to the handler for the next direction. Once a dog is comfortable negotiating singular obstacles on his own, sequencing at a distance should become easier.

With this thought in mind, this week's exercises may prove a bit difficult for some. Keep students from becoming discouraged by giving pointers on how they can improve their dogs' obstacle prowess. It would be best to backtrack if necessary and work on some singular obstacle performance exercises to check the ability level of the group. For the sake of this workbook, however, we will assume the foundation is laid and progress to discrimination and obstacle awareness exercises.

Remember, do not feel compelled to complete all of the exercises included here in one class. Help your students to maintain a positive attitude and, as always, find ways to improvise to insure success.

Organizational Notes

This is a good time to get an assessment from your students as to how they think everything is going for them with this training curriculum. You'll find that their satisfaction with the class is nearly directly proportional to the amount of work they have been doing at home with the Student Notes you hand out every week.

It's time to make a homework challenge. This week at home everyone should practice working their dogs on the weave poles at a lateral distance both on the left and right sides. They should practice calling their dogs through the weave poles. They should practice sending their dogs through the poles. Remind them to use a target when sending their dogs through the poles. Next week during class you will test everyone on how they are doing at working their dogs at a distance with the weave poles.

How to Conduct the Class

In a two-hour breakdown format this week's class would be conducted in this fashion:

- **First Period: Course Run**—Have all of your students run a course. Two suggested course sequences are shown in the Facility Layout. However, you can set any course that you like.

- **Second Period: Practice Sets**—You will break down the class into groups and practice the discrimination challenges in the different sets.

  Set 1 is The Terrible Twos, so named because it tests the dogs' ability to differentiate between two obstacles set 4'-6' apart. There is no rule as to which obstacles you place together. We have chosen the tunnel and teeter at random; feel free to make substitutions. Set 2 features the most commonly asked question on a competition course today: can the dog distinguish a tunnel from an A-frame or dogwalk? They are both obstacle discrimination exercises, one being slightly more difficult than the other.

  These two exercises could very easily be worked simultaneously if you have two instructors. Split the group in half and have each instructor choose a set to work. The objectives for success in each of these sets is quite similar, while the methods of negotiating them are quite different. In the lesson plan you will find detailed explanation of each set.

  Set 3 will be more difficult as it combines obstacle recognition with a turn. If you are using a two-hour class format, this set is best left for the second half of class with the group reunited. Explain once again that the object is for the dog to choose the intended obstacle himself, without the handler blocking the incorrect obstacle.

- **Third Period: Repeat Course Run**—The course that your students run at the end of this class can be the same course run at the beginning of the class, or it can be altered subtly to use the alternate discrimination obstacles from the practice exercises.

  In a one-hour format, you probably won't have time for running a course twice. You'll want to dispense with one of the two course runs, preferably the first so that your students can have the maximum amount of success from practicing the sequences.

Go the Distance

Week 4: Progress Worksheet

Instructors: **Date:**

Handler and Dog	Present	Notes

GENERAL NOTES:

WEEK 4

WEEK 4

Go the Distance

Week 4: Facility Layout

One square = 10'

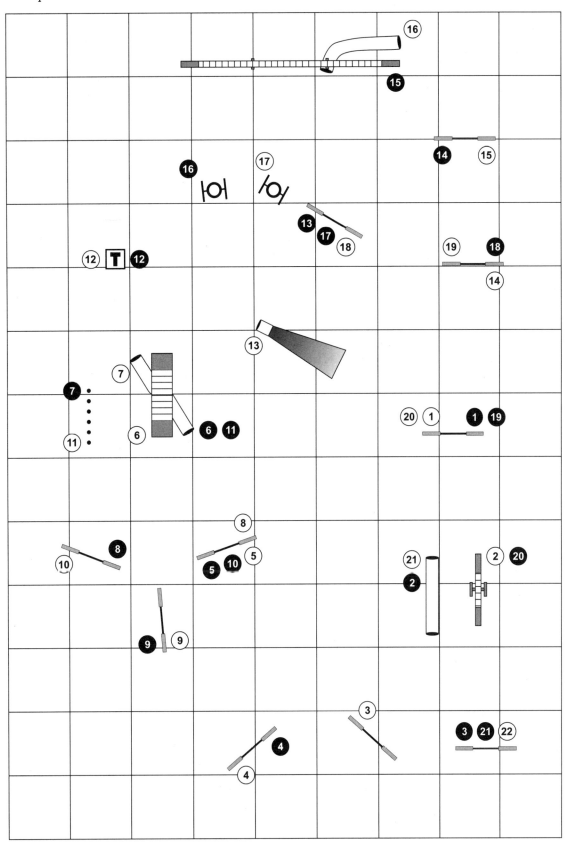

Week 4: Facility Layout Worksheet

Design your Facility Layout using a 1" = 10' scale (standard agility template)

Week 4 Exercises: Discrimination Breakdown

The goal of this week's lesson plan is to build confidence in both dogs and handlers, the outcome being greater discrimination skills and distance control, smoother handling, and a confident lead-out. Remind your students to allow the dogs to use their own abilities to solve problems. Problem solving is a key element in distance control. If a dog is confident and unafraid to try behaviors on his own, distance ability becomes inevitable.

Always remind your students that the easiest dog to train is a *thinking dog*. It would not be the purpose of these exercises to see how well a handler can block the wrong obstacle, or otherwise do the dog's job for him.

These initial training sets are a guideline to begin obstacle recognition and discrimination drills. The work doesn't end here. It *begins* here. Remind your students to be creative in coming up with future combinations and to make it both fun and interesting for themselves and their dogs.

Set 1: The Terrible Twos

The Terrible Twos exercises require at least two repetitions by each of your students. If you do one exercise followed directly by another without any repetition of each, it does not give the dog a chance to think through each exercise and make a conscious choice between the obstacles. The purpose of these exercises is to ask the dog to begin making thoughtful choices during a run.

Remind your students, however, that the main purpose of this exercise is to teach obstacle awareness, not distance. Also remind your students to not become discouraged if the dog is not racing away to the directed obstacle. As the dog's confidence grows, so will the distance. As the dog becomes more proficient at choosing the correct obstacle, the discrimination obstacles can be moved closer together.

The exercises are progressive. Each builds upon the previous to more complex obstacle choices. It is not a prerequisite that each dog and handler team be able to perform each set perfectly the first time. However, it is imperative that the goal be to always up the criteria. As a dog becomes successful at a certain point, be sure to increase the criteria the next time and reward accordingly.

Any number of obstacle pairs can and should be used to practice this set. A contact obstacle has been used in this set. You can substitute a simpler obstacle if need be.

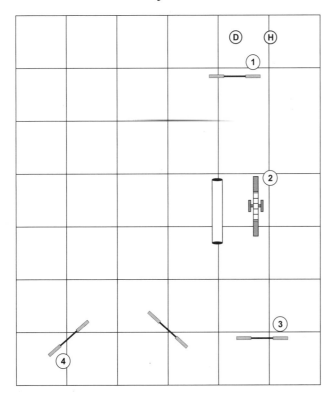

In the first sequence:

1. Place the dog behind jump #1.

2. Take a position lateral to the dog on the side favoring the teeter. This will influence the dog to take the obstacle on that side.

3. Send the dog over the jump and direct him to the teeter.

4. As the dog begins to approach the teeter, praise him and move forward to help the dog make the ascent. Reward the dog's willingness to go forward on his own and the attempt toward the proper obstacle.

5. Increase the send distance, allowing the dog to go further before indicating success.

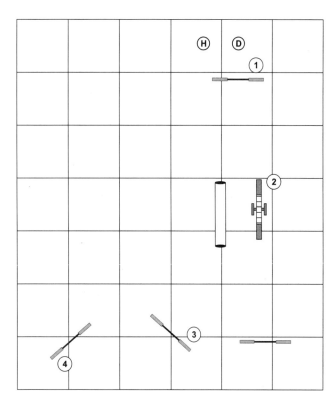

In the next sequence, the only real change is the obstacle following the teeter and the handler's starting position. The additional jumps at the end of the sequence are to encourage impulsion and aid in focusing the dog ahead of the handler.

1. Place the dog behind jump #1.

2. Take a position lateral to the dog on the side *away* from the teeter. This will test the dog's comprehension of the command to commit to the teeter.

3. Send the dog over the jump and direct him to the teeter.

4. As the dog begins to approach the teeter, praise him and move forward to help the dog make the ascent. Reward the dog with praise and a really good treat for going forward on his own and choosing the teeter.

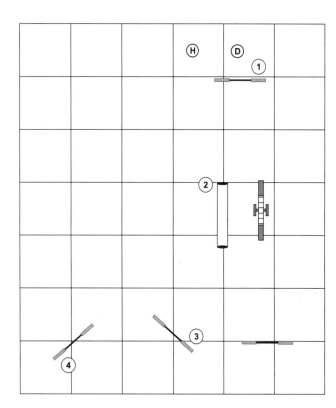

In the final sequence switch the obstacle the dog takes in the discrimination test.

1. Place the dog behind jump #1.

2. Take a position lateral to the dog on the side favoring the pipe tunnel. This position should be slightly exaggerated. This will influence the dog to take the obstacle to that side.

3. Send the dog over the jump and direct him to the pipe tunnel.

4. As the dog begins to approach to the tunnel, praise him and move forward to confirm his choice. Reward the dog's willingness to go forward on his own and to attempt the proper obstacle.

5. Increase the send distance, allowing the dog to go further before the handler indicates success.

Before releasing each group from this exercise, remind them that you have showed them a training method. You have not necessarily accomplished the training of their dogs. Each of your students must take personal responsibility to apply this training method on a regular basis to teach discrimination skills and to proof them.

Set 2: Triple Threat

The Triple Threat exercises push the dogs a step further, introducing a third obstacle, angled approaches, and complex obstacles into the discrimination grouping. With these exercises the goal is for the dog to make appropriate choices of obstacles. However, these exercises are more handler intensive. Your students should be prepared to use directional commands as well as body cues to ensure success. Blocking the wrong obstacle should not be considered as an option for negotiating these exercises.

In the long term, as the dog's fundamental knowledge and understanding of each obstacle and its proper negotiation begins to take root, the handler will become freer to focus on her responsibilities while the dog demonstrates his ability to do his job.

Allow everyone in the class to run the first sequence without specifying how the set should be handled. The entire class should watch their classmates perform the sequence. Incredible amounts of learning take place simply by observing others. It may help to identify potential problems or areas that may be simpler for one dog or the next before the sequence is even attempted. Ask your students to follow one after another, saving your comments until the entire group has attempted the sequence.

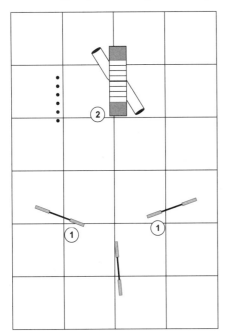

You may begin with either the jump on the left or the right. Instruct your students as to which obstacle should be taken after the first jump, the A-frame or tunnel. Instruct your students to run with their dogs to insure a true test of obstacle discrimination.

Observe your students' placement of the dog behind the first jump. After everyone has had a chance to perform the sequence, remind your students of the importance of a good set-up. If, for example, the desired sequence was left jump #1 to the A-frame, squaring up the dog on jump #1 would only hinder his ability to be successful as he would be looking directly at the weave poles over the jump.

The dog should be placed at an angle that presents the *desired* obstacle. It would be a good idea to instruct students to take a look at what the dog sees over the jump at various angles. This can be very enlightening for most people. A subtle change in the dog's position can often make the difference in the success of a sequence.

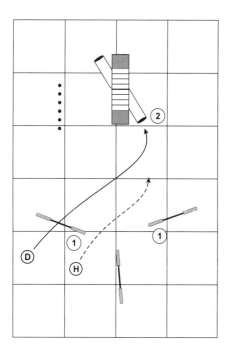

In the second sequence, switch the discrimination obstacle taken to the pipe tunnel under the A-frame. Tell your students to handle the discrimination as follows:

1. Starting with the dog behind the first jump, give the *Jump* cue.

2. As the dog completes the jump, do a slight shoulder roll to the right, drawing the dog in. Be careful to escort the dog *past* a square approach to the A-frame.

3. As the dog commits to this physical cue, give a verbal *Tunnel* command.

4. Reward the dog's willingness to go forward on his own.

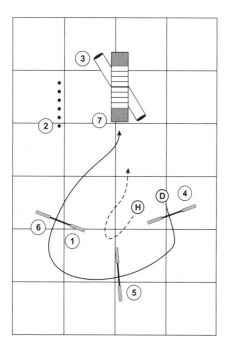

To add an element of difficulty, begin with the pinwheel of jumps to increase the dog's speed heading into the discrimination. This requires your students to address the discrimination in full motion, rather than from a static start. The discrimination obstacle taken will be the A-frame.

1. Run the indicated sequence.

2. At the pinwheel take a position on the inside, favoring an approach that keeps the dog on the left side.

3. As the dog completes the final jump in the pinwheel, do a slight shoulder roll to the right, drawing the dog in.

4. As the dog commits to this physical cue, give a verbal *Walk Up* command.

5. Reward the dog's willingness to go forward on his own.

Go the Distance

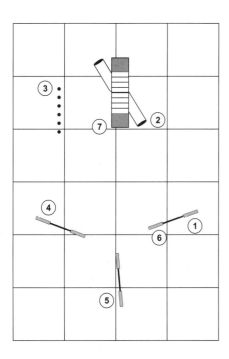

In the final sequence the discrimination is faced twice. Allow your students to compose their own solutions to this exercise.

Set 3: Trouble Around the Corner

The Trouble Around the Corner exercises introduce a turn to complicate the obstacle discrimination, followed by an additional discrimination if the tunnel is the obstacle of choice at #3. These exercises require a directional command and timely physical cues from the handler. Physical cues will either be a turn or a pivot. The necessity of a turn versus a pivot depends on the dog's impulsion and which of the two obstacles is desired.

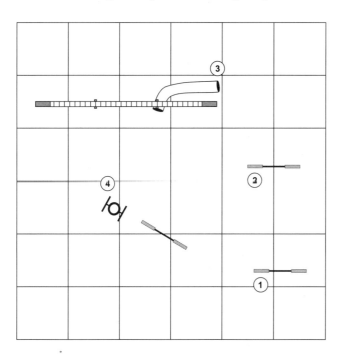

For the first sequence, advise your students to use this handling strategy:

1. Start with the dog, directing him over jumps #1 and #2.

2. As the dog commits to jump #2 begin to turn, directing the dog to the pipe tunnel. To get the dog into the pipe tunnel, give a fairly loose turn combined with a *Get Out, Tunnel* command.

3. As the dog exits the tunnel, issue a *Get Out, Tire* command.

Remind your students to keep an eye on the position of the dog to determine exactly where the turn should occur. If the turn is too early or too tight, the dog will naturally be driven onto the dogwalk. The turn should be performed at the point at which the dog is almost parallel to the tunnel entrance. The execution of the turn and the timing of the *Get Out* and *Tunnel* commands should be almost simultaneous so that as the handler is turning, the dog is peeling away from her side and heading for the tunnel.

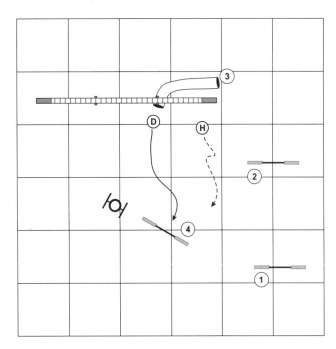

The second sequence changes the discrimination obstacle taken after the tunnel. Use this sequence to demonstrate how a reverse flow pivot (RFP) is used to direct the dog to the closer obstacle. The handler performs the pivot back against the path of the dog. This has the effect of tightening the dog's path into the handler. It is more compelling than *Come.*

1. Start with the dog, directing him over jumps #1 and #2.

2. As the dog commits to jump #2 begin to turn, directing the dog to the pipe tunnel. To get the dog into the pipe tunnel, give a fairly loose turn combined with a *Get Out, Tunnel* command.

3. As the dog exits the tunnel, do a reverse flow pivot to pull the dog away from the tire, then turn back and direct the dog to jump #4.

Tell your students to watch the dog's reaction to the pivot. Some of your students won't really believe in the pivot, and will supplement their handling with a frantic sounding *Come.* As an illustration for the nonbelievers, make them run the sequence again and tell them they aren't allowed to say anything when their dogs come out of the tunnel. Tell them to make their bodies do the talking.

NOTE: An RFP is a turn back *against* the grain of the dog's path. It has the effect of pulling the dog toward the handler's position. To the dog, the handler's turn indicates that he'll be going a new direction. As the dog pulls into the handler's position, however, the handler turns back and resumes the original direction.

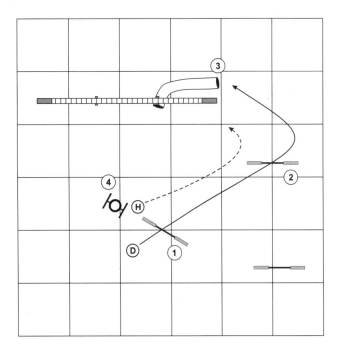

In this sequence the severity of the turn to the tunnel is increased due to the angled approach from jump #1 to jump #2. The rules for the turn are essentially the same as in the first sequence.

1. Start with the dog, directing him over jump #1 and #2. Make sure the dog is lined up for a straight run over jump #1 to jump #2.

2. As the dog commits to jump #2, turn tightly and direct the dog to the pipe tunnel. To turn the dog efficiently into the tunnel, it needs to be a tight turn.

3. As the dog comes out of his turn, issue a *Get Out, Tunnel* command.

4. As the dog exits the tunnel, issue a *Get Out, Tire* command.

Tell your students to observe the turn of the dog and the turn of the handler. The handler's turn will certainly affect the dog's turn. If the handler turns too sharply, the dog will get a good look at the off-course dogwalk. If the handler turns too loosely, the dog's turn will be lazy and loopy.

Go the Distance

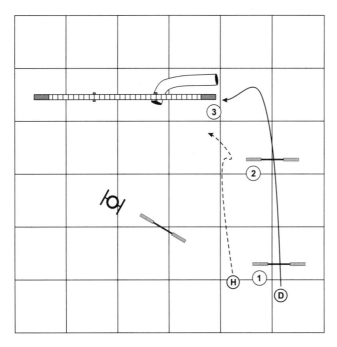

In the fourth sequence, the dog will be directed to the dogwalk rather than to the tunnel. In this discrimination choice, a reverse flow pivot or a much tighter turn is recommended. The RFP will work in the same way as the pivot in the second sequence you practiced. However, the steering must be more precise in this sequence.

1. Start with the dog, directing him over jumps #1 and #2. Make sure the dog is lined up for a straight run over jump #1 to jump #2.

2. As the dog commits to jump #2, execute an RFP and direct the dog to the dogwalk. Use a *Come* command to supplement the command implicit in the RFP.

3. As the dog tightens his turn toward the handler, turn and give a *Walk Up* command.

Remind your students of the importance of their physical position. The direction they are facing and the timing of the pivot influence which obstacle the dog chooses.

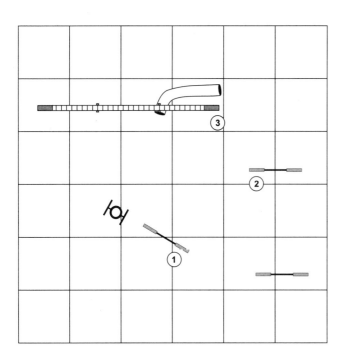

In the final sequence, the approach to the dogwalk is toughened by the angle of approach from jump #1 to jump #2. Allow your students to apply what they've learned using physical cues to solve this sequence.

To take this exercise one step further, you can do the same sequences without the benefit of physical cues. Use only the names of the obstacles to direct the dog. Repeat the same obstacle until the dog is consistently choosing the correct one, then ask for the other obstacle.

Remember to praise and reward generously for all successful conclusions! Be consistent in rewarding the small successes as well as the big ones. The small successes eventually lead to big successes.

Week 4: Student Notes

When things really start to click between a dog and handler in agility, something really magical happens between the two. They become a team. They work in tandem, smoothly and flawlessly, as though each reads the thoughts of the other.

The in-close working relationship of the agility team is extended to the at-a-distance game by the introduction of verbal cues that communicate the intention of the handler to the dog. In this sense the dog and handler develop and refine a language. The handler must learn clarity and timing; the dog understanding and responsiveness.

Sophistication of language is learned. And sometimes the learning is arduous. A child learns the language of his household only slowly, learning first only the most fundamental nouns to describe persons and objects in his immediate environment, and later verbs to describe the most basic actions. Facility in language comes from practice, conversation, consistency and reinforcement.

Developing a language between you and your dog also requires practice and conversation. Once you adopt a language basis, you must practice with the vocabulary. You must use it consistently and reward the dog for correct responses in order to reinforce the dog's understanding.

The two types of directional commands that you should teach your dog are *absolute* and *relative*. Absolute directionals are commands like *Left* and *Right*. These refer to the dog's left and right, regardless of your position when you give the command. Relative directionals are commands like *Come* and *Get Out*. The actions of the dog are dependent on (or relative) to your position. *Come* means for the dog to move toward you; *Get Out* means for the dog to move laterally away from you.

The two types of directional commands are not mutually exclusive. They can be taught to the dog, and taught at the same time.

Most important is that you practice this language of directionals, and practice a lot!

Tapping Mealtime Motivation

Before going further, it's important to understand how to apply the food treat. You really don't want to work a dog with a large amount of freshly eaten food in his stomach. Therefore you will reserve the greater share of the dog's dinner for the final repetition. On the first three repetitions the dog will get a small amount of dinner, a mere kibble. Then, on the final repetition the dog gets the jackpot balance of dinner.

They say you can train a food-motivated dog to do anything. At no time is the dog's motivation keener than at mealtime. So this is the perfect time to train, the perfect time to drag out those problem obstacles or to work on that tricky directional command.

In these homework exercises you will work multiple objectives with the dog. Each of the objectives represents an area where the dog needs work.

- Solid weave pole performance (good entry, no missed poles)

- Solid triple spread hurdle performance (keep all the bars up)

- Eager table performance

- *Go On* directional (continue straight ahead)

In this exercise you will have four stopping lines, which are numbered in the illustration.

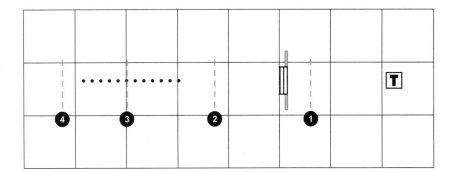

- In the first repetition you will escort the dog most of the way to the table, to line #1.

- In the second repetition, you will move only half way to the spread hurdle.

- On the third repetition you'll move only half way down the line of weave poles.

- In the final repetition, you'll send your dog away to do the entire sequence alone.

The exercise could be helped by a bait-master to remove the reward in case of any problem in performance. You do not want to reward the dog for running past any of the obstacles, or for faulting any.

Should your dog fault in any way, the exercise ends immediately, and the dog gets no reward. Return to the start of the set and try again.

Be consistent in using *Go On*. This directional means, to the dog, to continue in the same direction. That means that after the weave poles, you will say *Go On, Jump*. Then, after the spread hurdle, you will say *Go On, Table*.

Repeat the exercise for at least three mealtimes this week, and continue at every mealtime until your dog performs the four repetitions without fault. Work your dog both on your left side, and on your right. You should observe new speed, reliability, and confidence in your dog in the course of these mealtime training sessions.

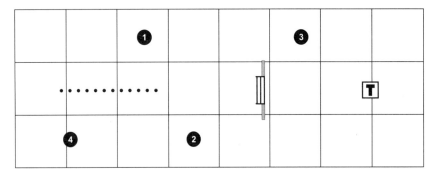

In this continuation of the basic exercise, you will vary your starting position in relationship to the dog. There are four different starting positions, which are numbered in the illustration. This is to vary the context in which you give the *Go On* command.

Remember that *Go On* means for the dog to continue in a straight line. It is an *absolute* directional. So it really doesn't matter where you are in relation to him as he moves. You should use no other directional but *Go On* to be consistent.

Repeat the exercise for at least three mealtimes. Continue at every mealtime until your dog performs the four repetitions without fault.

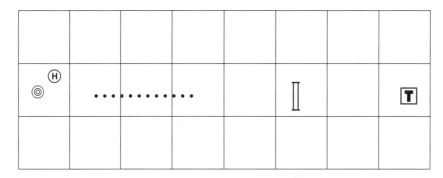

In this final exercise you will send your dog away from you to the table, and call him back to you or to a baited target. Start the exercise with bits of kibble on the table. Once your dog is reliably performing the sequence, give the reward only at the target on the return.

Repeat the exercise for at least three mealtimes, and continue at every mealtime until your dog performs the four repetitions without fault.

Verbal Cues for Directionals Without Physical Help

We will once again use the two-obstacle set for this week's progression. We are going to push the issue further and ask the dog to make the change of direction with a verbal cue alone. You may need the aid of your targets in the beginning, as the dog may initially have a bit of trouble going it alone. You are going to want to assume a neutral position with the obstacles for this exercise. The goal being to direct the dog verbally left or right over an obstacle and not influence the decision with your position.

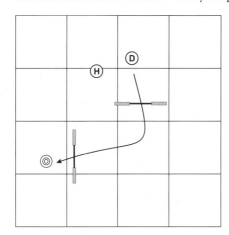

By this time your dog should not be having any difficulty sending to the first jump; the *Left* and *Right* commands should be an understood cue. However, removing the physical cue could be a momentary distraction for your dog. To increase the likelihood of success a target after jump #2 would be a wise idea.

After placing your target, position your dog in front of jump #1 and send the dog over the jump. As the dog makes commitment to the jump, instruct the dog with a verbal cue only to go left or right over the next obstacle. Release the dog to the target and praise.

Use the target for the first attempt in each direction. For each successive attempt go back to the toy or food tube to reward a job well done. You will find that, as your dog becomes used to the toy after the jump, he will become even more comfortable offering behaviors in hopes of a game.

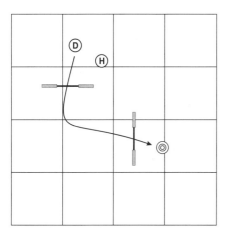

Do not be concerned if your dog begins to solicit for the toy before a behavior has been offered. Simply ignore the dog's attempts for a freebie. Work through the exercise and reward accordingly. The dog will understand very quickly that in order to get a reward it must exhibit the desired behavior first.

Week 5: Instructor Notes

This class is another step in the campaign to create a dog that will work reliably at a distance. Only part of your challenge will be to convince the dogs that it is okay to work at a distance from their handlers. The other, and maybe more difficult part, will be to convince the handlers.

One thing for sure, no one can run along with her dog as though they are stitched together in all Standard classes and games other than Gamblers, and then suddenly, in some 12-second window, come to a screeching halt and send her dog away from her to work. They have to *get loose*, in almost every context.

So much of Gamblers training is also about working loose. That means working with generous lateral distance to the dog, and staying out of the dog's space for performance of technical obstacles.

Jo Ann Mather

Aside from looseness in the team's working style, the handler must train her dog with a variety of repertoire skills. These are little directional tricks and cues, which help guide the dog through difficult passages.

The more obvious of these are simple relative directionals like *Come* and *Get Out*. Certainly *Left* and *Right* directionals would add a lot of power to the team's ability to maneuver apart.

Once a directional or other cue is taught to the dog, it has to be practiced on a regular basis. It has to become a part of the handler's working vocabulary with the dog. It has to be incorporated into training *and* competition.

Organizational Notes

You have to be ready to move some obstacles when conducting this class. In the transition from the lesson plan to the practice Gamblers match, you will need to set the joker as indicated by the numbered obstacles and the containment line shown in the Facility Layout.

Remember that last week you gave your students a homework assignment, to work on weave pole performance at a distance from their dogs. This week you should begin the class with a test, which is described in the exercise notes.

This becomes something of a competition. There really is no failing or passing. Some dogs take more readily to working the weave poles without being closely attended by their handlers. Some dogs just need more time and more encouragement. Use this as an opportunity to simply point out who needs to keep up with a good work-at-home program, and who is already doing a pretty good job with their program.

How to Conduct the Class
The class should be conducted in this fashion:

- **First Period: Group Exercise**—You will begin by testing each student on weave pole performance as described in "Group Exercise: Homework Review".

- **Second Period: Practice Sets**—You will break down the class into groups and practice the working sets which are dedicated to building the directional skill necessary to solve the riddle of the joker in the Gamblers game played at the end of the class. Rotate your students periodically between instructors, making sure to leave time to play the game.

  NOTE: The Swimmer's Cross (Set 2) should be taught *before* the Tandem 180° (Set 3), as the latter builds off of the first.

- **Third Period: Game**—Your students will play the game as described in "Playing the Game". It will be necessary to recruit a scribe, a judge, and a timekeeper for playing the game.

Week 5: Progress Worksheet

Instructors: **Date:**

Handler and Dog	Present	Notes

GENERAL NOTES:

Go the Distance

Week 5: Facility Layout

One square = 10'

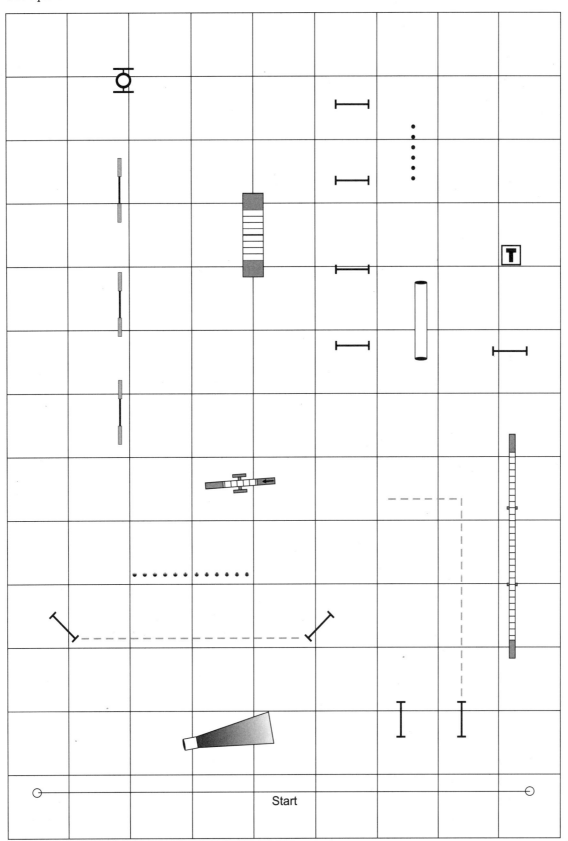

Start

Week 5: Facility Layout Worksheet

Design your Facility Layout using a 1" = 10' scale (standard agility template)

Week 5 Exercises: Gamblers

The goal of this week's lesson plan is to teach your students and their dogs a directional skill. The lesson especially demonstrates how the motion of the handler, rotation of the handler's body, and use of the lead-hand changes the way the dog moves in response. It is important to reiterate that the movement of the handler that makes a close-in game highly effective is equally necessary, or more so, to make the working-at-a-distance game highly effective.

The lead-hand can be generalized as the closest hand to the dog. It shows the dog what side he should be on, and points the way for the dog's path and choice of obstacles. The hand on the dog's side is used, because it helps the handler's shoulders stay square to the dog's path. A dog takes direction from the position of the handler's shoulders.

When the handler changes lead-hands, it becomes a signal to the dog that the direction of the course will change. This is a fundamental communication between handler and dog.

This lesson plan also introduces your students to the traditional Gamblers class. In addition, you'll be teaching a new and perhaps novel directional, *Back*, which is used to signal the side change during execution of a rear cross.

Working a dog at a distance is not all a matter for the Gamblers class. Distance work allows a handler who might be slower than her dog to work the dog at some speed and distance while she takes a more casual and shorter path.

Group Exercise: Homework Review

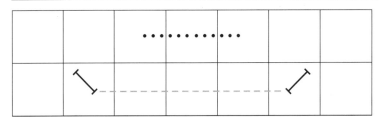

In last week's homework assignment students were assigned the task of working weave poles at a distance. Give everybody a chance to show what they've accomplished with their dogs at home during the past week.

Set up two jumps and a set of weave poles as shown in the Facility Layout. Work the dogs through this sequence, jump-weave-jump. Do it left to right, working with the dog on the heel-side. Then work the sequence right to left, working the dog on the off-side.

At the first sign that a dog is reluctant to perform the weave poles at a distance from his handler, instruct the student to step in and supervise the dog's performance of the poles. The exercise should end on a positive note.

Set 1: Skills Review

This lesson plan builds on previously trained skills that are important for a successful conclusion. The lesson plan begins with a review of these skills:

- Send to the table.

- Working a complex obstacle at a lateral distance.

Send to Table

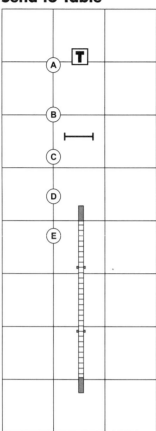

In previous weeks your students have practiced sending their dogs to the table. This exercise adds a new element. The send-away will follow performance of the dogwalk.

This exercise requires the services of a bait-master who will place a tasty food treat on a target at the back of the table, away from the dog's line of approach.

For dogs not ready for this send-away, a modest start by backchaining the sequence is required. If the dog is sufficiently food motivated, backchaining will go relatively quickly. The letters "A" through "E" in the illustration indicate the point at which the handler releases the dog to the table in the backchain series. Letters can be skipped if the dog quickly understands the drill.

The operative directional should be *Go On* as the handler releases her dog toward the table. To the dog, *Go On* means to continue in the direction he is moving.

For dogs ready for the send to the table, the handler should stop the dog in the contact and then give the dog a push to the table, remaining behind while the dog goes ahead. The handler may need to take an initial step forward to release the dog from the contact. The arm signal to the jump should be made rather like a bowling motion, starting low to get the dog's attention and lifting up to get the dog's head up to see the jump.

Complex Obstacles

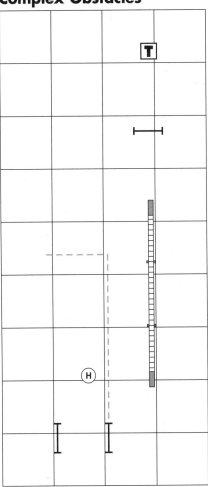

In this exercise the handler remains behind the containment line. The sequence is two jumps, dogwalk, jump, and finish on the table. The dog should already be keen to go on to the table in anticipation of the treats placed on the table in the previous exercise. However, in this exercise there will be no bait on the table. Your students should give a reward to the dog *after* the complete performance.

Again, the operative directional should be *Go On* as the handler releases her dog toward the table.

It's important not to allow the dog to fail. If the dog absolutely can't stand for the handler to remain behind, then the handler must move in and direct the dog to both the final jump and the table.

Roger Brucker

Set 2: The Swimmer's Cross

One of the greatest challenges in working a dog at a distance is changes of direction. This lesson focuses on a unique relative directional command, *Back*. This command, as used in this exercise, is like a two-part directional.

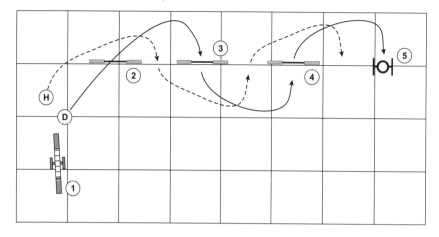

This exercise gives practice in crossing behind the dog and using the off-arm signal, the nonverbal equivalent of *Get Out*. As the handler steps in behind the dog, she will call him to *Come* and then redirect him to the next jump. Rather than mixing up *Get Out* and *Come*, use the *Back* command here. This will hopefully develop as a verbal cue for the dog to continue to turn, rather than continuing in a line, as suggested by *Get Out*.

Restrict your students to the handling method described here. This exercise isn't about how they would solve the sequence. It is about learning the off-arm cross. Follow these steps:

1. Start with the dog on the right and have the dog take the teeter and jump #2.

2. As the dog clears jump #2, encroach onto the dog's path, sweeping around with the left arm in a lead-hand change. The command *Back* should be given as this move is made. If the handler uses a *Come* command, it should only be after she has crossed behind the dog to tighten the dog on the turn to jump #3.

3. As the dog clears jump #3, cross again, with a change of lead-hands to the right hand. Note that the handler will cross on the landing side of the jump.

4. The turn to the tire is a bit trickier. The handler needs to allow the dog to turn a little wider in order to get a clean entry to the tire. As the dog clears jump #4, allow the dog to take an extra stride or two. Then cross with a change of lead-hands to the left hand.

Note that the handler comes very aggressively into the dog's path. This motion helps to train the dog to bend his path away from the handler.

The greener the dog, the more likely that the dog will *not* have a nice turn in tandem with the handler. The green dog may initially turn the wrong direction. This is nothing to be alarmed about. The dog will soon learn that the handler's *Back* command means "I'm coming over", and will make the turn with the handler.

Some handlers actually cause the dog to turn the wrong direction because they hesitate at the corner when they should be coming across aggressively. There should be no hesitation when turning the corner. The dog will take great pains to scoot out of the handler's way. Indeed, the aggressive motion becomes a learning tool for the dog.

Another problem some handlers have is cocking back the new lead-hand before making the lead-hand change. This is confusing to the dog as the initial motion is going the wrong direction. There is no need to cock back the new lead-hand. It needs to push out abruptly, with no signal to the wrong direction.

A faster dog with a wider turning radius could actually be compelled by the handler to run past and turn, missing the next jump in line. The handler of this dog must learn to shorten her curve to help keep the dog's curve shorter. For example, the illustration shows the handler's path centered between the line of jumps. The handler of the dog with a longer turning radius would take a path closer to the previous jump. That is, on the approach to jump #3, the handler would tuck up very close to jump #2 during the turn.

Set 3: Tandem 180°

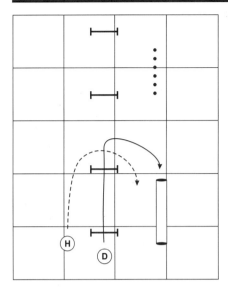

This exercise involves a simple cross behind the dog, building on the work done from the previous exercise (The Swimmer's Cross). The Tandem 180° occurs on the landing side of a jump.

The handler's command as she's making the cross is *Back*. At the same time the handler will switch lead-hands. In this case the right hand starts the sequence, showing the desired path and each of the two introductory jumps. While making the cross, the left hand comes up in a broad sweeping motion to signal the cross and change of sides.

You will find that a very green dog may turn the wrong direction initially, coming off the turning jump. This is a green dog error only. With a sufficient number of repetitions the dog will learn to turn in the same direction as the handler, so that the two of them execute a pretty synchronous turn during which the handler changes working sides with the dog.

Training with a toy can be useful for some dogs to help them get the turn. The handler should have the toy in her off-arm hand. When coming across into the dog's path, the handler throws the toy. Once the dog starts to understand the implications of the new lead-hand coming up, and anticipating the toss by turning away, the handler must start to hold the toy for a moment and then toss it in the new direction, 180° to the original path.

Handlers should do this exercise starting the jumps in either direction in order to practice both right and left *Back* turns to the pipe tunnel. They should not progress until the dog is turning with the handler and appears to understand the significance of the handler's crossing motion, the change of lead-hands, and the *Back* command.

In all of the variations of this exercise the handler must lead out enough so that she will be pretty much at the dog's side at the moment of the turn. This will depend upon the speed of the individual dog, and may require some experimenting to get the timing right.

Complex Cross

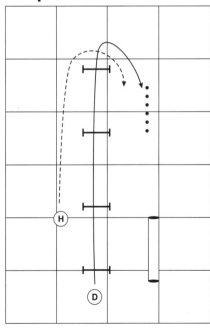

In this exercise the handler will execute the *Back* turn into the performance of a set of weave poles. This is a slightly more difficult exercise than the basic cross in that the weave poles are a complex obstacle. The previous exercise has prepared the dog for the turn. The handler must still be attentive to getting the dog lined up to see the weave poles, before giving the command to *Weave*.

Note that in this exercise the dog won't really know where he is coming out of the line of jumps. It will either be after two jumps or four jumps, depending on whether the approach is to the pipe tunnel, or to the weave poles, and depending too on which direction the line of jumps is started.

Handlers should practice this exercise starting the jumps in either direction to practice both right and left *Back* turns to the weave poles. They should not progress until the dog is turning with the handler and appears to understand the significance of the handler's crossing motion, the change of lead-hands, and the *Back* command.

When the dog is getting the significance of the cross and the *Back* command, it is time to begin putting some distance between the handler and the dog.

Adding Some Distance

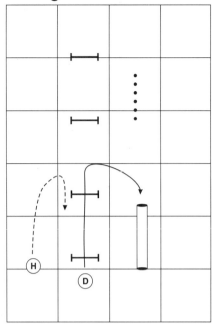

This exercise assumes that the dog is turning away from the handler, and reversing direction at the handler's crossing motion, change of lead-hands, and use of the *Back* command. The big step the dog and handler are taking is that the handler will not complete the cross, and will remain a distance from the dog.

Note that the handler starts at some lateral distance from the dog. This allows enough room for the handler to take a step into the dog, adding an encroaching motion to the multiple cues the handler is providing the dog.

The handler has to make a judgment call. If the dog doesn't get out and back for an approach to the pipe tunnel, then the handler must abandon the plan to stay on the original side of the jump and push the dog out for the approach. The handler can then step back on the other side of the jumps to finish at the greater lateral distance.

Remind your students to make a big deal out of a successful conclusion to the exercise. Give the dog a lot of praise, a favorite treat, or a game with a toy.

Handlers should practice this exercise starting the jumps in either direction to practice both right and left *Back* turns to the pipe tunnel. They should not progress unless the dog is turning away from the handler promptly so that the handler does not have to cross the line of jumps.

Complex at a Distance

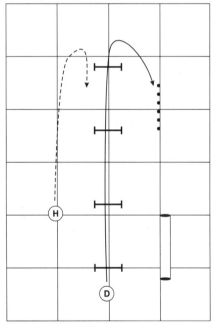

This is the most difficult exercise in this series. Not only must the dog perform the *Back* turn, but he must enter and complete the weave poles at a distance from the handler. Dogs and handlers should not progress to this exercise unless they are having clear success with the previous exercises.

Again the handler starts at some lateral distance from the dog, allowing enough room to take a step into the dog, and adds the element of encroaching motion to push the dog out and back.

If the dog doesn't get out and back for an approach to the weave poles, the handler must abandon the plan to stay on the original side of the jump and push the dog out for the approach. The handler can then step back on the other side of the jumps to finish at the greater lateral distance.

On the approach to the weave poles the handler also should pay attention to the dog's line. If the dog is running too wide, the handler needs to call the dog in. If the dog's line of approach is too shallow, the handler needs to give the dog a *Get Out* to the poles.

Reward a successful conclusion to the exercise with a lot of praise, a favorite treat, or a game with a toy.

Handlers should practice this exercise starting the jumps in either direction to practice both right and left *Back* turns to the weave poles. They should not progress unless the dog is turning away from the handler promptly so that the handler does not have to cross the line of jumps.

Playing the Game

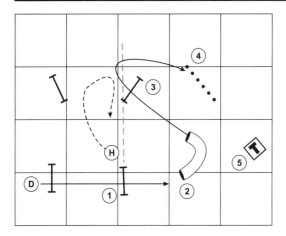

End the class with a Gamblers practice match. The illustration shows the configuration of the joker. You'll have to move some equipment to set this. Enlist your students to quickly get everything in position for the practice match.

Before playing this game it's important for you to set your students' expectations. You've started them on a training path. But one simple session is unlikely to have the dogs trained and proofed. If they don't successfully complete the gamble at the end of point accumulation, it is not the end of the world. Some will very likely successfully perform the gamble. Stranger things have happened.

Give 30 seconds for the point accumulation period. Give up to 20 seconds for successful completion of the gamble. At this stage of the game a successful sequence at a distance is more important than pushing for time. Use a 1-3-5-7 point system. Give 7 points for successful performance of the teeter.

Time permitting, you might want to talk about some of the strategies of the Gamblers class. Here is a quick list:

- Look for opportunities to practice in the opening sequence the handling required by the gamble. Consider the two-jump approach to the tunnel.

- While walking the course, determine the best strategy for point accumulation that will have the dog on the approach to the gamble when the accumulation period expires.

- Use back-to-back performances of high-point obstacles to minimize time spent on transitions.

- Don't play tight to the dog through the point accumulation period and then expect the dog to shift gears into distance work to do the gamble.

Analyzing the Gamble

After allowing your students ten minutes to walk this course and develop their own handling strategy, you should talk to them about their strategies. It's a good idea to allow students to provide their own analysis of the gamble.

Following are some additional notes for your use:

- In this gamble the biggest mistake the handler can make is to move away from jump #1 while the dog is in the tunnel. The handler's motion helps communicate flow to the dog. The movement would be wasted if the handler uses it up while the dog is in the tunnel and can't see the movement. So, the handler should stay still at the spot designated "H", then push forward on the indicated path as the dog emerges from the tunnel.

- Handler and dog maintain a parallel path. The handler must *not* indicate the change of direction until the dog is committed to jump #3. Then the handler pushes to kick the dog *Back* to the entrance to the weave poles. A timely command to *Weave* will help the dog.

- As the dog clears the final pole, a timely *Go On* then *Table* command should keep the dog from turning back away from the table.

Go the Distance

Week 5: Student Notes

Certainty is the most powerful training tool. The certainty of reward or correction provides the dog with the fundamental input to reason through the desired performance and to learn.

Cherie Gessford

Nothing is required beyond certainty. The trainer does not have to babble or scowl or flap her arms; she does not have to yell, or cry, or yank and poke. Indeed, all of these activities confuse the dog and interfere with his ability to reason through the desired performance. These antics prevent learning.

We submit that a correction is a neutral act. It is not administered in pique or anger. It is a helping hand to point the dog in the right direction. Reward, on the other hand, is always a positive act. It is food, a quick game, or praise; all acts that reinforce the dog's behavior or performance in a happy context.

Monitor yourself for inappropriate correction. Many failures are handling errors, and not something the dog did willfully. Most dogs will gladly do what you ask, if only they understand what they are being asked to do.

Be consistent both in the application of praise and *neutral* correction. Some handlers will be so bound up by their own egos, sadly more interested in looking good in front of the other students, that they neglect those times when praise, a tasty treat, or a game with a toy would reinforce a specific performance. The reward is an important teaching tool. It tells the dog that he did right and makes it much more likely that he will do right again when presented with the same challenge.

Working Off the Dog's Left and Right

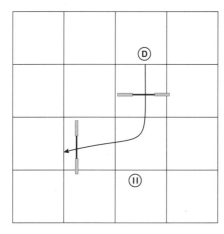

For this exercise you will be required to call upon your skills in determining left or right based on the dog's position. Remember *Left* and *Right* in the context that we are using them dictate that a dog go a certain direction based on one verbal cue and the other direction based on a separate verbal cue.

1. Position the dog in front of the first jump.

2. Lead out 12' or so beyond the jump.

3. Turn and face the dog.

4. Call the dog over the jump. As the dog commits to the jump begin your turn and give the respective *Left* or *Right* command.

Be careful as you monitor your timing for this set that your command is not too early. This could easily cause the dog to drop a leg as he negotiates the change of direction and take down a rail.

Several repetitions of each direction are recommended. Let the dog be the indicator of how many times to repeat the exercise.

Have the dog's toy ready, as this is another example of an exercise that would be well served by instant reward at a distance. Asking the dog to perform the *Left* and *Right* directionals with you facing him should not be a problem as long as you use the correct cue.

Obstacle Names for the Discriminating Dog

Some say that only a small percentage of dogs truly understand the names of obstacles. Yet, we all run along using them from obstacle to obstacle. *Go Jump, Tire, Weave, Table*, we chant. But, we've all seen the handler in competition who errs by stating *Go Tire* when the next obstacle is actually a tunnel. So, what did the dog do; stop and go looking for the tire? Of course not, he took the obstacle in front of him without a second thought.

What happens when the same dog is presented with a tunnel and a tire in close proximity? Suppose the handler gives no greater clue than just the verbal cue *Go Tire*. What happens then? Chances are it's dog's choice. The dog will obey some subtle nonverbal cue without respect to what his handler actually says.

These proofing tests don't so much prove the dog's inability to actually learn the names of obstacles. They really indicate how little effort we put into teaching them.

Here's an obstacle recognition training method used by several of the top agility trainers in this country. Put two obstacles alongside one another. Use an A-frame and a tunnel, for example.

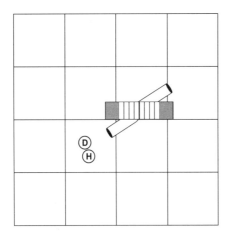

1. Hold your dog about 5' away from the tunnel.

2. Tell him *Tunnel... Tunnel... Tunnel...* The instant he looks at the tunnel, release him to go through.

3. Reward him with praise and a treat or a game with a toy.

Note that you start by placing yourself on the same side as the obstacle you want him to perform.

Roger Brucker

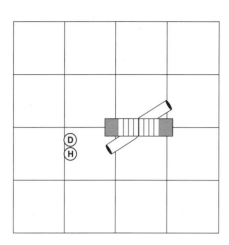

Now, as your dog really starts to appreciate the game, start adding some complexity to it. These are the complicating conditions:

- Vary the dog's angle of approach to the obstacle.

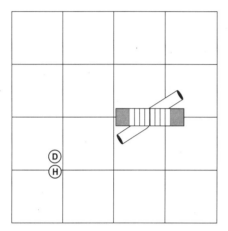

- Vary the dog's starting distance from the obstacle.

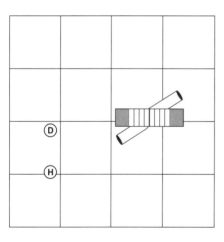

- Vary the handler's position relative to the dog before releasing him to the obstacle.

Only after the dog has mastered the first obstacle can you start teaching the second obstacle.

Then you'll want him to completely master the second obstacle before you begin to randomly alternate which obstacle you are sending him to perform.

Obstacle Vocabulary

Do you have too many obstacle names in your vocabulary? For example, have you named every contact obstacle separately? Do you have different names for different types of tunnels? Do you have a variety of commands for a variety of types of jumps?

It could be that you should simplify your dog's vocabulary, limiting your working vocabulary to match the different actions you require of the dog. This would simplify the task of teaching obstacle name recognition.

Obstacle	Current Command	Simplify to...
A-frame	*Scramble*	*Walk Up*
Dogwalk	*Walk*	
Teeter	*Teeter*	
Single bar jump	*Jump*	*Jump*
Spread hurdle	*Big Jump*	
Long jump	*Over*	
Tire	*Tire*	
Pipe tunnel	*Tunnel*	*Tunnel*
Collapsed tunnel	*Chute*	
Table	*Table*	*Table*
Weave poles	*Weave*	*Weave*

Week 6: Instructor Notes

Agility is a funny game. We approach it very seriously with compulsory exercises, and training regimens, and all sorts of complex and technical terms. Yet, in the final analysis, agility is nothing more than a game that we play in the park, on weekends, with our dogs.

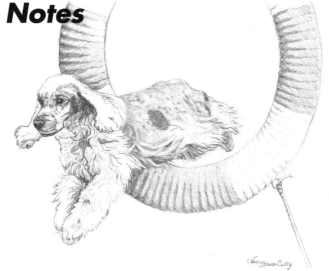

Class-time training is only in small part intended for the benefit of the dog. The instructor doesn't speak to dogs. She speaks to the human member of the agility team. Indeed, it's the instructor's duty to coach the handler to train her dog. The instructor has an eye not only for performance, but also for the relationship between each dog and handler in class.

So, if agility is really only a game, then the instructor must constantly be directing her students to that realization. When they get *that,* they'll own the most fundamental key to unlocking the dog's motivation and teaching the dog to learn.

This distance stuff is really not so important in the grand scheme of things. But more than one handler has been enchanted by the dream of standing in the middle of the agility ring, calmly directing the hurrying dog through an entire course with a pointed finger and voice command. Oh, you know the related dreams too. The handler dreams of beaming as she collects her blue ribbon and qualifying ribbon, to the applause and the roar of approbation from her admiring peers. And there's the dream about the interview on Animal Planet, where she tells the whole world how she trained her amazing remote-control pooch.

You, the instructor, have the pleasure of being the middleman on your students' quest for greatness. You are the mentor that will continue to put positive thoughts into her head and infinite words of wisdom into her training vocabulary. It is your ability as an instructor along with her ability as a trainer that will guide the team down the road to success. You must find the way to keep the fun in agility for your students during the training process. It is very difficult at times for her to remember that perfection is not always necessary to be successful. This message must be conveyed in such a manner that coincides with her interview on Animal Planet.

Average human beings are always going to try their best to block out the messages that they do not wish to hear. This is inevitable when in training you are forced to contradict the student's preconceived notion of how it is supposed to work.

These are circumstances beyond your control.

Organizational Notes

These are complex exercises with the advanced dog and handler in mind. Feel free to modify any or all of the sets to meet the needs of your class. However, keep in mind that the goal is to increase your students' ability to work laterally away from their dogs. So, be sure that in any modification, the original purpose is not overlooked.

There are suggestions throughout each set description explaining how to increase the level of difficulty. Because your students should not be expected to work through the progressions in one or two sessions, these are guidelines that can be used for future training sessions or worked at home.

This class uses a relay as the featured game. Instructions for running the relay are included at the end of this chapter.

The illusion with this lesson plan is that it requires a very big field, and can only be conducted by a tunnel-rich club or training center. This is only an illusion. Each of the exercises in the lesson plan uses essentially the same obstacles which can, with minimal movement, be reset from one exercise to the next.

How to Conduct the Class

The sets are progressive and will be best worked in order. If you are dealing with a one-hour class, you may need to spread the lesson plan over at least two weeks. It is best to keep the group together as it helps a great deal to watch others in learning the proper execution of this command. Encourage students to critique one another after the completion of the sets, monitoring the handler distance. For example, pay attention to whether the handlers are returning to the centerline, or are they crowding or following their dogs too much? This can be of great benefit, as the handler is distracted by and thinking of the mechanics of the exercise.

Time is a big factor in any group training. Consequently, you will want to keep the number of repetitions of each set to one or two, with the exception of Set 4. For this particular set, three or four repetitions may be necessary to obtain the full benefit of the exercise. You will also want to explain to the class that these sets may cause the dog to question his own performance if asked to perform the sets too many times. In some instances, repetition is not always the key to success. Remind handlers that it is their responsibility to monitor their dogs' ability to repeat an exercise after successful completion. You always want to end a training session with success.

Week 6: Progress Worksheet

Instructors: **Date:**

Handler and Dog	Present	Notes

GENERAL NOTES:

Go the Distance

Week 6: Facility Layout

One square = 10'

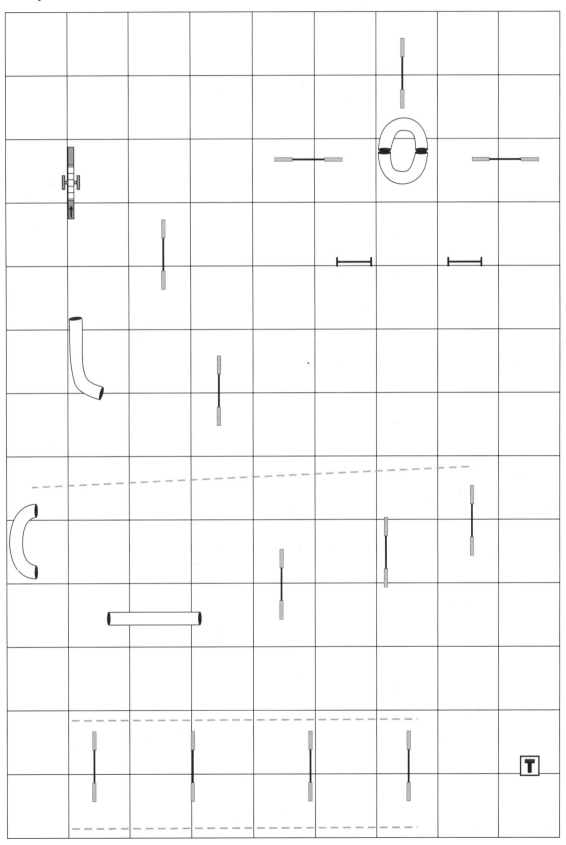

Week 6: Facility Layout Worksheet

Design your Facility Layout using a 1" = 10' scale (standard agility template)

Go the Distance

WEEK 6

Week 6 Exercises: Get Out Relay

As the instructor, you have the dubious honor of being expert, motivator, and cheerleader. Be careful to monitor your students and help them feel positive about their progression. The potential level of difficulty in these sets could become stressful at times, so remember to reward your students for even the smallest of successes.

The purpose of this week's lesson plan is to build on the fundamental understanding of the *Get Out* command started in an earlier class. This directional command is an integral part of distance control on all types of agility courses from games to standard titling classes.

When we think of distance control, usually the first thing to come to mind is *send distance*. Of equal, if not greater importance to your success on the field is *lateral distance*. This is where the *Get Out* command plays such an important role. This command is what links the dog's ability to properly negotiate an obstacle with the ability to do so at a distance from his handler.

The sets for this week's lesson concentrate solely on that goal, assuming an understanding of proper obstacle performance has already been established. Set 1 is a general layout designed to demonstrate very clearly to both dog and handler what constitutes a *Get Out*.

Sets 2 through 4 test the dog and handler's ability to combine the *Get Out* with other course challenges such as turns and more complex obstacles such as the teeter. We will also explore the difference between the *Go On* command and the *Get Out* command.

In Set 4, we are teaching the difference between a *Go On* and a *Get Out*. The following analogy works great in explaining the difference: We look at a straight-line sequence and automatically assume it to be a *Go On*. However, we are mistaken, given the fact that a dog's head steers its body. As the dog proceeds down the line, it will be necessary for him to turn back to see the handler. This pulls the dog's head to the left or right, which now becomes the direction he is going and often the dog will turn in that direction. This behavior is frequently mistaken for defiance on the part of the dog when, in actuality, the dog is absolutely correct. The *Go On* command is a generic "take what you see in front of you" directional that can easily be misused by handlers if they are not careful.

Set 1: Out, Out, and Away

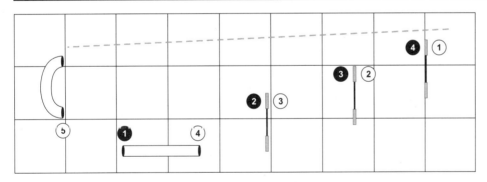

This is a progressive exercise where one or two successful attempts is all that is necessary before increasing the difficulty factor. Once the dog has done the exercise, the object is to gradually increase the dog's lateral distance capabilities while the handler maintains a straightforward path. The line is to note the position that the handler should always return to upon issuing the *Get Out* command. The handler should issue a verbal command as well as use a sweeping sideways arm motion (using the arm closest to the dog) and step into the dog's space. Rather than repeating the same exercise, have the handler move the line out 6" or so at a time upon success at the previous distance. This process should continue until the dog is no longer successful, at which point the line should be replaced to the position where the dog and handler were last successful. Repeat one more time to ensure the dog's ability to negotiate the sequence and stop there.

One of the crucial elements in successful negotiation of this set and the others is the dog's knowledge of the various obstacles by name recognition. The handler will be running along side her dog; however, a key element in the dog's learning of the *Get Out* command is the handler's ability to overlay the *Get Out* with an obstacle name.

This helps to ensure success by associating a familiar with an unfamiliar. As the dog's knowledge of the *Get Out* command increases, you will be able to use it without the secondary obstacle command when necessary.

When teaching the *Get Out* command, it is essential that you push the dog out and then return to your own centerline. The centerline is the straight path you are attempting to take while the dog goes out laterally to perform the desired obstacle. If you move with the dog as you exclaim *Get Out,* you will only be teaching the dog that when that command is used, you'll *both* be heading in the designated direction. This defeats the purpose of *distance control* altogether. The centerline gives the handler a definitive point to come back to and ensures proper position with a little less difficulty for the handler. Please remind your students that the centerline is not a gamble line. It is a handler aid to simplify the exercise. They may cross the line and most likely should when issuing the command. However, the goal is to be back on the other side after the command is given.

Timing is incredibly important in this exercise. The next command should be given as the dog extends over each jump and before he exits the tunnel. The *Get Out* comes first and is followed immediately by the obstacle name, almost as if they are one word.

The obstacles should be set initially in such a way that, if positioned properly, the dog can see straight down the middle of the jumps and into the tunnel. This is a good place to start with a less experienced dog, keeping in mind that the goal is to teach the dog how to *Get Out* to an obstacle or obstacles. You must instruct handlers to resist the urge to set their dogs at the start in such a manner that they are looking directly down the line. Instead, have them position their dogs squarely in front of the first jump, not at an angle, so that the dogs do indeed have to look out to find the next obstacle. The dogs will very quickly pick up on the sequence, which will only help the handler's cause, as the command will still be issued and the dogs will be successful from the start!

A lead-out may be warranted for the handlers of more driven dogs so that the handler maintains a reasonable position to the dog. Lead-outs require a solid understanding of the *Stay* command, a *must* for any agility competitor.

After moving the line laterally to increase the distance, the next progression is to stagger the obstacles more so that eventually, the straight line connecting the obstacles disappears. You may want to add perpendicular jumps between jumps #1 and #2 and jumps #2 and #3 to add a new challenge. One other variation would be to add a cross between the tunnels so the handler switches sides and uses the *Get Out* command on the way back down the line.

For the dog that is too Velcro for the entire exercise, don't be afraid to backchain the obstacles. Start with the last jump to tunnel sequence and work back toward the first jump upon success from the third, and second, and so on. Be careful not to lose sight of the point of the exercise, which is to create the ability of the dog to maintain lateral distance away from the handler.

NOTE: The most space consuming of the exercises might be Set 1, which calls for a minimum distance of 90'. This can be modified to a 65' or 70' long set for the *small universe* training area by leaving out the tunnel at #5. The set would have the same objectives, and look like this:

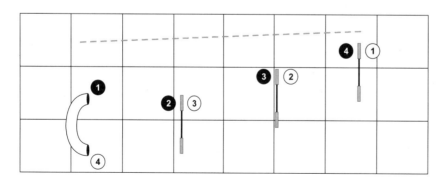

Set 2: The Pill Bug

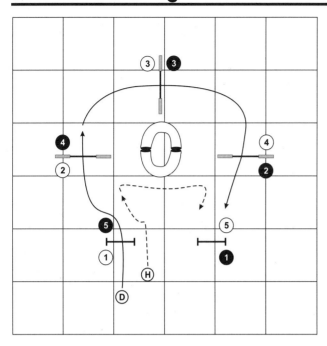

This set is designed to test the dog's ability to *Get Out* with an obstacle restriction. Initially, you may want to make the exercise simpler by setting jump #3 so that there is no room between it and the tunnel.

The set also adds another new challenge to the *Get Out* concept with the inclusion of a turn.

Remember to use both verbal as well as physical cues to provide the dog with the most information possible.

This set may pose some initial problems with the addition of the tunnel in the middle. Make sure the handler gives timely cues, allowing the dog a chance to work it out. Don't be in too big a hurry to help the dog unnecessarily.

You may start the circle going to the left or right.

The handler should position the dog in front of one of the approach jumps. She'll then direct the dog over the jump and go with the dog past the initial jump, while directing the dog over the next jump and out and over the next, continuing until the dog completes the circle.

As the handler directs the dog over jump #2, an immediate *Get Out, Jump* should follow as the handler turns 90° toward jump #3. Repeat this for jumps #3 to #4. The handler should be careful to monitor the dog's position in relation to the jumps so as not to turn too early and pull the dog in, or too late and push the dog out too far. It is the handler's responsibility to read the dog's position to maintain proper timing of cues, both verbal and visual.

Make sure that the handler is turning to face the direction of the appropriate jump as the dog moves from one jump to the next. Ideally, the handler will follow a path parallel to the obstacles being performed.

If the dog balks at a jump or tries to go around a jump, a quiet *Wrong* should signal the dog that a different behavior is expected. Allow the dog the opportunity to try to solve the problem, remembering to have a party with the dog upon successful completion of the set.

Be sure to run the exercise in both directions and deal with any sidedness issues that may be evident.

The next step is to start distancing the jumps from the tunnel and repeating the process. As with the previous set, avoid too many repetitions at the same stage. For example, as the dog becomes proficient in going left with the jumps up against the tunnel, stop there and switch directions. When the dog is successful going to the right as well, increase the spacing. Each dog will have a greater threshold for repetition and length of concentration on one specific set.

Be careful not to allow your students to treat this exercise like a gamble. Remind them to avoid coming to an abrupt halt before the first jump in the pinwheel. The handler should keep moving even if it means running in place. For the less driven dog, the movement of the handler, even if only in place, may mean the difference between a successful or unsuccessful attempt.

Set 3: Perpendicular Peril

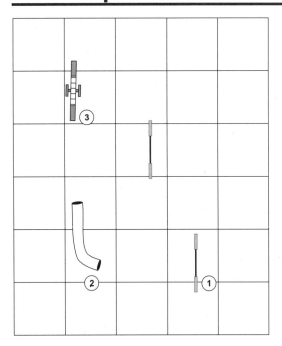

This set adds a dummy jump as a handler restriction. You will also note the introduction of a complex obstacle, the teeter, in this set.

This exercise would be best presented to handlers as a problem-solving issue such that everyone (instructors and students) reserves comments until all students have tried it once. Allowing students to think it through initially should enhance the learning process.

This set is fairly straightforward with emphasis on the *Get Out* as well as the dog's ability to properly negotiate the teeter at a distance from the handler. To obtain the full value of this exercise, the handler should plan on executing the three obstacles from the outside of the dummy jump.

This set will introduce the handler to more effective use of body language in association with verbal cues. As the dog exits the tunnel, he should have already been given a *Get Out, Teeter* while the handler is positioned perpendicular to the teeter.

When the handler teaches a dog to read body language, she should expect the dog to follow a path parallel to her and take the obstacle she is parallel to at any given time. Therefore, by assuming a perpendicular position to the teeter, the dog should respond by turning out toward the direction the handler is indicating. This combined with the *Get Out, Teeter* command will send the dog out far enough to align himself with the teeter. Then, when the dog has gone out far enough, the handler should turn to indicate the teeter by assuming a position parallel with the obstacle.

Once again, you must remind handlers that timing is of the utmost importance. A handler's timing should be determined by the dog. As with previous sets, no more than one or two repetitions are necessary on these exercises. Once the dog has successfully completed the set, repeating it unnecessarily could confuse the dog by causing it to think that it is wrong and thereby cause it to seek out incorrect alternatives in an effort to be correct.

Remind your students that although this week's lesson is designed to teach the *Get Out* command, proper obstacle execution must not be overlooked. This becomes more prevalent with the use of the teeter in this set. If the dog is unable to successfully negotiate the teeter at a distance, instruct the handler to close the distance once the dog has begun the obstacle and gradually increase the distance from the teeter at another time.

You could also use a target beyond the teeter to entice the dogs to continue moving in a straight line.

Roger Brucker

106

Go the Distance

Set 4: To *Go On* or To *Get Out?*

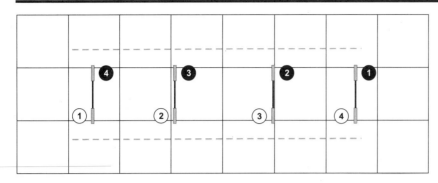

This set is designed to answer the question is it a *Go On* or a *Get Out?*

No lead-out is permitted on this exercise.

Ask your students to negotiate this set the first time without your input.

The handler should be on the other side of either line with the dog positioned in front of jump #1. The handler releases the dog over the initial jump with a *Get Out, Jump* due to the fact that she will begin with a lateral send.

Ideally, treat this set as a gamble-type exercise to enhance the understanding and differentiation of a *Go On* and a *Get Out.* The whole class can be brought together to work this set. A round robin approach works well to minimize downtime for students.

A great way to run this set is to ask students to initially use a *Go On* command down the line of jumps and immediately repeat it in the other direction using *Get Out.* The purpose of reversing direction is to avoid a pattern training response from the dog. The object is to show students that it is the head that steers the dog and he will go in the direction he is facing. As the dog gets further ahead, he will turn his head more to check in. As this happens, the dog is no longer looking forward and the next obstacle is now to the left or right as opposed to straight ahead of the dog. A *Get Out* becomes necessary to redirect the dog's attention straight ahead instead of remaining to the left or right of the line of jumps.

This set could be repeated two or three times from each side. Keep in mind the number of students and available class time. Ask each individual to be ready to go as soon as the handler in front of them finishes her turn.

Set 5: Happy Table

The *joker* or distance element of a Gamblers class will often end at the table. It is the obstacle that stops time. The dog should be keen to seek out the table and hop up on it when commanded. Unfortunately our training is too often contrary to this simple goal. That is, we load up the table with emotional baggage. Or, the table represents a stop in play for our dogs. Most dogs would much rather be in motion than sitting or lying down.

This exercise then is geared to getting our dogs into a happy frame of mind when approaching the table. At the same time, we can work on a simple *Go On.*

This exercised is backchained. A bait-master is required. Collect a bag full of all the dogs' treats so that there are lots of goodies to make the table a happy place.

Start by presenting the dogs one at a time to the table. The handler should walk right up to the table, give the *Table* command, and point out the treat sitting on the table.

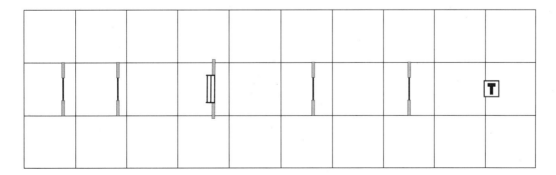

In the next repetition the handler will send the dog to the table from a modest distance, say 6' or 8'. The bait-master can point to the treat on the table.

Now, one jump at a time, the handler will back up and send the dog from an increasing distance to the table. The dogs will quickly understand the reward implicit in the game and will hurry to get to the table and the treat.

If a dog turns back toward his handler, the handler should quickly step in and show the dog the table and the treat. This handler should start the next repetition closer to the table, and backchain the sequence again.

Running the Relay

Form your class into teams of two or three. Design a relay course, which reflects many of the working challenges of the day. Use a baton, and require that the members of the team exchange the baton as each in her turn runs the same sequence. You'll need a timer to capture each team's overall time.

Add faults to the team's time. Use whatever schedule of faults you feel is reasonable for your students (for example: 5 faults for a dropped bar, 20 faults for an off-course, refusals not faulted).

The illustrated sequence is one possibility, using one of the working exercises for the relay.

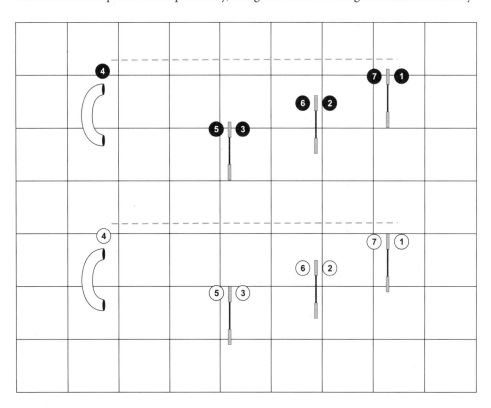

The interesting thing about any relay is that when you put a baton into the hands of the team, they are transformed. You get three very quick sequences. If your students were asked to run the same sequence individually, it would take at least twice as long to get through the same sequence. So the baton becomes a device to keep the class moving along.

If you have enough time, run the relay a second time at the end of the class.

Week 6: Student Notes

How far should you be able to send your dog away from you to jump? The answer to this is quite simple: The length of your backyard!

Training a dog to go away to a jump is quite simple really, even if you have what's referred to as a *Velcro dog.* You start very close to the jump, bop your dog over, and reward him lavishly with praise, treats, or his favorite toy. Then you start backing away from the jump for longer and longer sends.

Nancy Krouse-Culley

The distance you back up is a matter of how much your dog can deal with. The more clingy dog will need you to back up in modest increments. The inspired and highly motivated dog will allow you to back up in bigger chunks. It is your obligation to increase the distance of the send in exactly the right increments so that the dog never really fails. When the dog clearly *gets it,* you'll know; and at that time you can back away from the obstacle some more.

This game also works for tunnels, the table, and almost any obstacle. It also forms the basis of a pretty fun game of puissance, which can be played by only two dogs and their handlers. Each of you back up more and more, sending your dogs away to the jump until one of the dogs fails to negotiate the jump at the final distance.

Go On

A command to complement the *Left* and *Right* commands is the command *Go On.* Its name implies its meaning exactly, go on to the next obstacle. *Go On* tells the dog to continue to move ahead, taking whichever obstacle he sees. This command is not a necessity, but can enhance the effectiveness and reliability of *Left* and *Right* by giving them more definition.

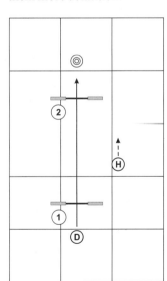

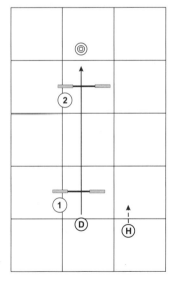

Last week's 90° jumping sequence will be replaced by two jumps in a line.

1. Place the dog in front of jump #1, lead out between jumps #1 and #2.

2. Call the dog over jump #1.

3. Direct the dog to the next obstacle with a *Go On* command followed by the name of the obstacle.

A target placed after jump #2 is helpful.

The next step would be to send the dog over both jumps with you positioned behind them. This will again call for the use of a target.

Remember for the next step, to replace the target with a toy or food tube being tossed over the second jump after the dog commits to it.

Toy-Motivation

A dog keen to play with a toy is ripe to learn and will do almost anything for a proper game with that toy. The dog will show you his best speed for his toy. You are tapping into his prey drive and his play ethic. That's where his best effort and motivation lies.

But you have to understand the rules of the game: You don't set the rules, the dog does. Once *you* set the rules, it's no longer a game. It's work, and no longer deserving of the dog's best speed and effort. So, let the dog set the rules. For example, *his* game might be throw and catch. It might be keep-away or tug-of-war. Whatever is his game, *you* be a good student and learn that game. Don't get caught in the cycle of wanting some kind of retrieve (that would be *your* game, not *his*), as though you had some kind of obedience agenda to fulfill.

Now let's say you've set a goal of getting your dog to do super fast weave poles at a distance from you, without any errors (improper entry, missed pole, and so on). Use *the game* as reinforcement and reward.

Start this training with a simple performance of the weave poles. Immediately as the dog clears the final pole, play the game. Toss the toy and play *his* game.

Make the game a bigger part of the activity than the work on the weave poles. Too often we, the hairless ape with a dour work ethic, put too much emphasis on work and not enough on play. The dog will no more enjoy doing five minutes of weave poles for one minute of play than you would enjoy five days of work for one day of pay.

If the dog faults the poles during this training, you are to withhold the game. This is a neutral action. Don't get mad or otherwise abusive. Or, the next time you approach the poles, the dog will see through your thinly disguised ruse to make this work appear a game. When you withhold the game, you have the option of either allowing the dog to restart the poles or putting the toy away for another time.

Over time you can use the game, playing with a toy as a reward, to up the ante on the performance of the poles. For example, if he does all the poles, but with not nearly the speed he is capable of, only play the game for a half-minute or so. On the other hand, if he really zings the poles doing them as fast as he can, you should really get excited and play the game with him for five minutes or so. The significance of the application of this value system will not be lost on the dog. Dogs are smart that way. You just have to be consistent.

A Dog Can be Taught Toy-Motivation

Sometimes a dog will appear indifferent to any kind of toy. This is often true of dogs who live with more domi-nant toy-motivated dogs. They never get a chance to get or have a toy, so never develop much drive to try. Some dogs, even if they are the only dog in the house, will be indifferent to toys. However, they can be taught.

Take the dog to a place with no other distractions, no food, no other dogs or people, no interesting smells. Keep him on a leash, perhaps secured to your belt to free your hands. You are the center of activity. Now, *you* play with the toy. A ball, dangling on a rope from a stick, is ideal for this kind of activity.

Play, play, and play. If the dog shows any kind of interest, tease him with the toy. Play keep-away, skittering the toy just out of reach so the dog has to lunge to get at it if he wants to get involved in your game. If he captures the toy in his mouth, play tug-of-war or wrestle with him playfully.

Let the game develop naturally. Let the dog make the rules. In time, you will have a supremely toy-motivated dog that looks forward to playing with you and his toy with great relish. In building that toy-motivation you have created a reward system to be used for training the dog.

Week 7: Instructor Notes

There will be dogs that will not leave their handlers' sides. These dogs are frankly not ready for this more advanced lesson plan. In the students' homework assignment are prescriptions for getting the dog accustomed to distance work in the privacy of one's own backyard. However, if a dog will not send 3' over a jump, it is unlikely that the dog will be ready very soon for a lesson plan this advanced. It's not a good idea to tell a student that her dog will *never* be able to do this kind of work. Part of your job is to be encouraging to your students.

Nancy Krouse-Culley

But you can tell her that her dog isn't ready yet. If they must work with this group and in this class, you should advise these problem students not to fret the distance work, to work each sequence for the at-side performance, and to think about putting modest distance between themselves and their dogs as they work.

Part of the reality of running a training center as a profit-making endeavor is to keep everyone motivated and directed for the training. You are both a cheerleader and a mentor. But if the training agenda is too much for either the dog or the handler, you really have to make a call that very likely will remove them from the training program.

Be very sure about your call. It could be that your student isn't doing her homework. You can usually tell these things in class. And of course you could settle the question by asking your student. So, should you remove a student from the training program for not doing homework? It certainly is a possibility. Included in the homework in this workbook is a solid eight-week program for teaching a dog *Left* and *Right*. If your student has ignored these lessons, the dog will certainly not be ready to respond to these commands in class or in competition. A dog does not *have* to learn *Left* and *Right*. A dog and handler team can have plenty of success with relative directionals alone. In the Student Notes there is also a wealth of training tips for these relative directionals. However, if that homework too has been ignored, there is not much to commend this student for a program teaching distance work. It just isn't going to get done by dragging the poor animal to class once a week.

Be careful what you tell your students. Don't underestimate your influence upon them. If you tell them they are going to do great if they have patience, or if you tell them they'd better drop out because they are doomed to fail... they will remember. So, be very sure about your call.

Organizational Notes

Be sure your instructors have read and understand this entire lesson plan. They need to be prepared with objectives and remedies to conduct a successful class. There's a lot of good material here that can be repeated *verbatim* to your students.

The game format for this week's instruction will require the employment of a timekeeper, a judge, and a scribe. You can either draft your instructors, or mix the jobs up among your students, having them to do the jobs when another jump height is engaged in the game.

This is a good time to pass out the homework assignment. Point out the exercises in the homework asking them to figure out their dogs' yards per second (YPS). Tell them this is an assignment. They must come to class the next week each knowing their dog's YPS and their own pace divisor.

Some students will complain that they never know what dog they are going into the ring with. "Sometimes my dog is fast and sometimes my dog is slow. I never know what dog I'm going to be running." Listen to them patiently and then penalize them for complaining by assigning them the task of calculating *two* YPS figures: one for when their dog is slow, and one for when their dog is fast.

In addition to the working sets, you will play the game Jokers Wild with your students. The purpose of this game is mostly to allow them to have a bit of fun, and to experiment with some of the distance skills they've been working on over the course of this class. The rules for Jokers Wild are summarized at the end of this chapter.

How to Conduct the Class

The working sets should be practiced first. Save enough time at the end of the class to play the game. Every dog will have 55 seconds on the course. You should allow about a half minute between dogs. So the amount of time you need to save for playing the game should be easy to calculate.

Divide the class into two groups, one instructor to each group. One group should work on Set 1: Split Decision while the other group works on Set 2: Teeters Away and Set 3: The Verelli Gambit. Then combine both groups for Set 4: The Calls To.

Timing will be fairly important. Therefore you should adjust the timing of the Calls To exercise to give yourself exactly the right amount of time to finish the class on time with every dog having run in the concluding game.

If you are working a one hour class you should divide the lesson plan over two weeks.

Week 7: Progress Worksheet

Instructors: **Date:**

Handler and Dog	Present	Notes

GENERAL NOTES:

Week 7: Facility Layout

One square = 10'

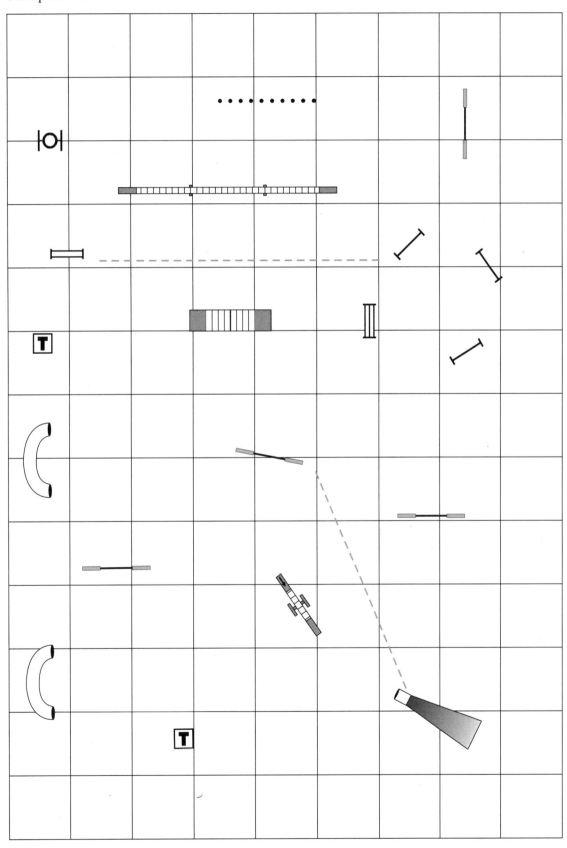

Week 7: Facility Layout Worksheet

Design your Facility Layout using a 1" = 10' scale (standard agility template)

Go the Distance

Week 7 Exercises: Jokers Wild

Today's lesson plan deals exclusively with performance of the complex or technical obstacles, which include the weave poles and all contact obstacles. This is possibly the most straightforward type of distance work to learn. The difficulty arises from the way dogs are initially trained to perform the complex obstacles. The handler insists that she must be crouching and hovering over her dog throughout the performance of the obstacle. She convinces herself that it is her micro-management that makes or breaks the performance. Unfortunately, this can be a self-fulfilling fact, until the handler finally trains the dog to appreciate that it is okay for the handler to stand at a distance during the performance of the obstacle.

Much of today's lesson plan is dedicated solely to the objective of prying apart the handler and the dog. You can tell your students that the idea is for the dog to be comfortable working at a distance from his handler. Keep in the back of your own mind that it is an equal challenge to convince the handler that it is okay to work at a distance from her dog.

Set 1: Split Decision

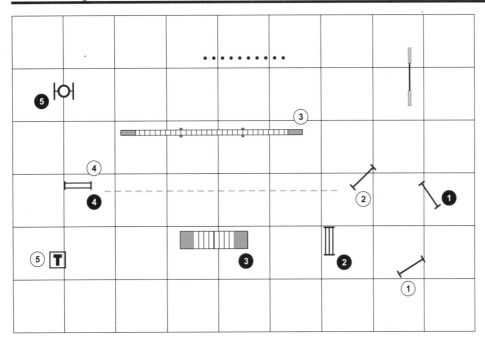

This is a two-part exercise. Do no more than four or five repetitions of the white numbered sequence. Then do four or five repetitions of the black numbered sequence.

Tell your group that it's not a good idea to over-drill these exercises. It would be better to quit on a positive note after only three or even two repetitions. Some dogs may take drilling to mean that they are doing something wrong. This might make them confused and leave the team with more of a performance problem than they started with. This is not desirable.

Contacts are not the most important element of this drill. By the same token, you don't want students to ruin their dogs' contact performance. There are two remedies for a dog that is missing contacts in either sequence:

1. Use an action command that the dog is likely to understand. For instance, on the approach to the contact obstacle the handler might say *Easy* if the dog understands that command. On the descent of the obstacle the handler could use a command like *Lie Down*. Even with the handler at a distance the dog should respect this command.

2. Bend the line. The handler might want to get in a bit closer to the dog to enforce the contacts. Then gradually back off in successive repetitions.

It is important in this exercise that the dog gets out to make the ascent without thinking too much about whether the handler is in close attendance. So, for each of the two sequences, the handler should square up the dog for the opening jumps and make the approach to the contact obstacle at a run. Depending on the dog's speed, the handler may want to take a lead-out. How much of a lead-out really depends on the speed and natural impulsion of the dog—a lot for a fast and motivated dog—a little or none for a slow dog.

If the dog will not get away from the handler to make the ascent, the handler needs to bend the line. It's every handler's own responsibility— not the instructor's—to know at what distance the dog is working comfortably. The instructor should urge students who are obviously putting too much distance between themselves and their dogs to bend the line in closer to the dog. And, being a true devil's advocate, suggest putting more distance between handler and dog when the advice seems warranted.

Other advice that will help you with this set:

- Keep moving. One of the fundamental laws of working a dog at a distance is that things will break down any time the handler stops. Your students will want to stop while their dogs are approaching the descent side contact. This could cause the dog to bail off the side, toward the handler.

- Tell your students to use an action command for the contacts.

- Tell your students to use their hands to focus the dog's path. This is not only true of the opening jumps, but is true of the final jump as well. If the handler is lollygagging parallel to the dog, there is a good possibility that the dog will run by the concluding jump.

Set 2: Teeters Away

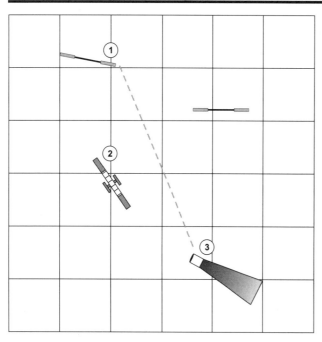

Make sure that you read the Instructor's Notes for Set 1. Much of that advice applies equally to this exercise.

Since there is only one jump before the teeter, it is the handler's responsibility to get the dog moving smoothly in the direction of the first jump. Make sure the dog is lined up so that the teeter is clearly framed over the opening jump. There should be adequate room prior to the jump to get the dog going. A handler standing flat-footed at the beginning of the distance challenge is an invitation to disaster.

The command to get the dog to the teeter should be crisp and well-timed. It should be repeated until the dog has gained the ascent. *Walk Up, Walk Up, Walk Up* or whatever command an individual student uses for the teeter.

Remind your students to keep moving on a parallel path to their dogs. Bend the line if the dog is hesitant about working a distance away from his handler. Instruct your students to use a verbal command to the tunnel while the dog is still on the plank to direct him forward off the plank. Instruct them to use a good hand signal to the tunnel to finish the performance.

Set 3: The Verelli Gambit

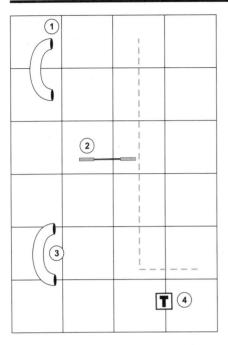

This set actually comes from a USDAA Advanced Gamblers class judged by Tim Verelli in Columbus, Ohio in June of 1998. It's a delightful distance challenge puzzle. The dog has to go into the right side of tunnel #1. However, Tim stipulated that the dog could enter either side of tunnel #3.

Let your students run this at least once before you give them any input to the strategy and handling. What's not immediately evident about this sequence is that the table is framed in the dog's vision over jump #2 while he's coming out of tunnel #1. If the handler merely pushes the dog straight over the jump, there's a good possibility the dog will never see tunnel #3, or be turned back to it only with great difficulty and arm flapping on the part of the handler. Of course some handlers will pull it off successfully by giving the dog a strong *Get Out* after the jump, or just the command for the tunnel. But most will not.

The objective of this exercise is to teach the handler to think about modifying the dog's path when the possibility to do so exists. In this case, the handler needs to draw the dog back to the handler's line coming out of tunnel #1, and then turn the dog to jump #2 with such an approach that tunnel #3 is framed for the dog over the jump.

Repeat the exercise once or twice after you have explained the handling strategy to your students. Remind them that the best practice in any distance challenge is to always find a way to keep moving. A handler standing flat-footed is always courting disaster.

The illustrations show step-by-step movement of the handler's path and the dog's path.

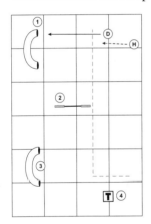
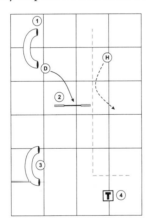
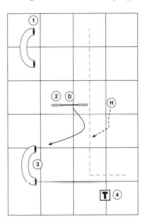
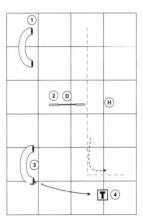

Set 4: The Calls To

In this exercise collect your students into one big group. The number of repetitions for this exercise may be increased or decreased based upon how the timing of previous exercises has gone. Remember that you'll want about half an hour for 12 students for the final game. Adjust the timing of this exercise accordingly.

The importance of teaching a dog to perform complex obstacles at a distance cannot be overstated. You will certainly see these types of gambles in competition. And when you do, if you have prepared your dog adequately, you will take home the qualifying ribbon.

You must teach a dog the complex obstacle performance in every context. The exercises in this lesson so far have been focused on parallel path performance, that is, the dog and handler are moving in the same direction, parallel to one another.

In this exercise ask your students to:

1. Pick any obstacle on the field.

2. Leave the dog in a stay.

3. Move to the opposite side of the obstacle.

4. Call the dog to perform the obstacle.

Do two or three repetitions with any single obstacle, then move on to another obstacle to repeat the performance.

Remind your students that it would be highly desirable to perform the weave poles and the contact obstacles in this fashion. But tunnels and jumps should also be included in this exercise for balance.

Have no sympathy for the handlers whose dogs will not stay for them as they lead-out to do these exercises. Do not allow students to hold each other's dogs. It's far better that they suffer for this lack of training immediately, and without a crutch, so that they will perhaps go home and do some actual stay training.

Playing Jokers Wild

This game is very much like the traditional Gamblers game. There are some not so subtle differences: most restrictions are removed.

Your students will have 55 seconds to accumulate points. At 40 seconds a whistle will blow, allowing them to attempt an on-course joker (the Verelli Gambit) one or more times in the final 15 seconds. The competitor may, instead, continue to accumulate points as in the first 45 seconds.

When the second whistle blows at 55 seconds, point accumulation ceases. The team with the highest score wins.

Scoring

- Competitors have the option to carry a *doubling base* onto the field. At any time in the run they can put the base down in a strategic position. At a time of their choosing they may elect to stand on the base. All points earned while standing on the base are doubled. Once the competitor leaves the base, however, it may not be used again.

- Any negative verbal reprimand to the dog will result in the loss of 10 points.

Obstacle	Points	Doubled
Teeter/A-frame	5	10
Weave Poles	7	14
Jumps	1	2
Tire/Tunnels	3	6
Negatives	-10	-20
Joker	50	100
Dogwalk	0	0

Week 7: Student Notes

Some of this is going to seem immediately like a math assignment. However, we're going to ask you to figure out some very useful numbers which will help you become more successful at the game called Gamblers.

What's Your Dog's YPS?

Artist: Chris Lewis Brown

First of all, let's define our terms here. The acronym YPS means yards per second. This is an important statistic in dog agility because it refers to your dog's working speed over a set of regulation equipment. It's easy to figure out. You can figure it out yourself, or use statistics that already exist from competition (usually better than trying to figure it out yourself).

- Determine the course distance (CD)—This is usually announced by the judge prior to a Standard class and written on the posted scoresheets.

- Determine your course time—This is written on your scribe sheet and on the posted scoresheets.

- Determine your running time (RT)—This is the course time minus five seconds for the table count (if a table was used on the course).

- Divide the course distance by your dog's running time. The result is your dog's YPS.

For example, suppose the judge says the course was 180 yards and you finished the course in 55 seconds. That means that your dog's YPS is 3.6. Remember, the formula is CD/(RT-5).

What's the Length of Your Pace?

The purpose of this exercise is to determine an accurate and even measurement for your pace.

To determine the length of your pace, find a reasonably long line of a reliably measured distance. A football field would work fine. You know that it is 100 yards long. Start at one end and walk in a natural and relaxed pace to the other end. It's *important* that you use a natural pace and not try to force your step into a one-yard average. This will be too difficult for you to try to maintain for an accurate measurement when you are called upon to use your pace for the purpose of measurement.

Do the math:

- Walk the length of the football field (or whatever known distance you are pacing out).

- Count your steps

- Divide the known length by the number of paces

- The result is your divisor

For example, suppose you walked the football field counting 115 paces. The formula is 100/115 = .869

Applying Your Divisor

Here's where it gets fun. Let's say your dog's YPS is 3.6. The judge gives you 30 seconds for point accumulation. That means that your dog will work pretty close to 108 yards during the point accumulation, assuming that you are keeping up a brisk working pace as you would in a Standard class.

In a Gamblers class you can use the course walk-through period to pace out that exact distance. So, if your divisor is .869 you would divide 108 by .869 to arrive at the conclusion that the path you pace out should be around 124 paces.

Send to Jump

It's absolutely crucial that your dog is willing to send away from you to perform agility obstacles. The number one challenge and the most obvious is to send your dog away from you to jump. Since we all have jumps in our backyards, this is an exercise which you must begin doing immediately on an almost daily basis, if you aren't doing so already.

Use treats or your dog's favorite toy. Reward your dog for going over a jump. Start by working with your dog at side. Then, gradually *stop* going all the way to the jump with your dog. You'll quickly learn exactly how far away from you your dog is willing to work.

The biggest danger of this exercise is that *you* will want to progress too quickly. Keep in mind that every failure—as in the dog won't go all the way to the jump—is like taking two steps backwards. It's your job to gradually increase the distance to the jump so that the dog will never fail. This is really difficult. It's a fact of human nature and ego that *we* are ready to progress as soon as *we* are ready, and may be tempted to do so, without full understanding of what our canine partners have actually learned.

If you are pushing so fast that you are failing every other turn, then you're not helping your dog.

Directed Recall

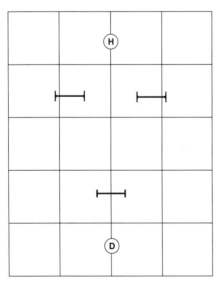

This is a simple exercise intended to help your dog learn to watch you when doing a recall. You leave the dog in a stay. Then you call the dog over, and indicate one jump or the other. Alternate which jump you are directing the dog to.

Don't get hung up on performing this exercise in the formal and restricted style of the obedience competitor. To indicate the direction the dog should turn after the first jump, it is better to half-twist your body toward the jump rather than standing like a department store mannequin holding up one hand stiffly. The timing of your turn can be important. If you turn too early your dog may pull off the first jump, following the turn of your body.

It should be very obvious that you cannot do this exercise, or any recall at all, if you don't have a reliable stay on your dog. So if this is a problem for you, you should put a lot of work into teaching your dog to stay.

Without belaboring the training method, the key to teaching a reliable stay is the certainty of correction. But please don't use any harsh or negative correction. Harsh training only damages your dog's sense of fun. That is counter-productive in agility training. Just remember, if you let your dog get away with breaking a stay, then you have reinforced the behavior. This is not desirable.

More of *Go On*

For Week 7 we are going to increase the difficulty factor for the *Go On* command by adding two jumps and creating a jump square. Please note the distance between jumps #3 and #4 in relation to jumps #1 and #2. In this exercise we are adding peripheral distraction to help the dog better understand the concept of *Go On*. We are not trying to stump the dog.

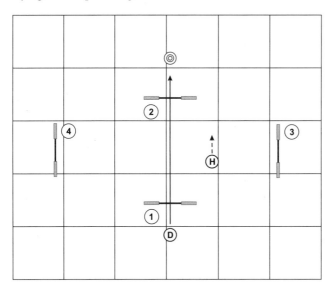

Repeat the process from Week 6; begin with a lead-out between jumps #1 and #2 for the initial send. It is also recommended that you use the targets for the first attempts.

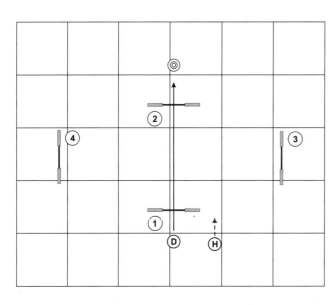

Follow this by remaining behind both jumps and issuing a *Go On* command between jumps #1 and #2, followed by the cue for jump #2. Remember to replace the targets with the toy or food tube.

If the dog attempts to turn to take one of the unintended jumps, a soft *Wrong* should be sufficient in asking the dog to try again.

If the dog continues to turn after the first jump, go with him a few times to reward the desired behavior, then try the distance again. Two or three successful repetitions are plenty.

Week 8: Instructor Notes

This is the final lesson in a curriculum designed in eight tidy chunks. On this day you may graduate your students, if you are inclined to such ceremony.

Cherie Gessford

This is a time for taking stock, for evaluating how the training worked for your students and your instructors. Make a record of your observations and insights. This *learning* will improve the delivery of these lessons next time, allowing you to make improvements, and avoid mistakes.

This is not the end of the road. For many of your students, who somehow survived the application of these lessons in working a dog at a distance, it is only the beginning. They'll take their new-found skills and training direction with them into the show ring, into their daily practice. Some of them may surpass your own achievements in competition; some won't.

What you have really achieved is to show your students the possibilities, and to arm them with the training objectives for distance work and the training steps to accomplish those objectives. It is now up to your students to integrate what they have learned into the training relationships they have with their dogs.

The authors of this book would very much like to hear of your experiences with this lesson plan. What worked? What didn't work? In what ways can we make the presentation clearer?

The simplest way to contact the authors is via email. Feel free to contact us at the following Internet addresses:

- Stacy Peardot: agiljack@aol.com

- Bud Houston: dogwood1@compuserve.com

Organizational Notes

In this final class we will play a game called Timed Jumplers. The rules of this game are described at the end of this chapter. You will need a scribe, a timekeeper, and a judge. The scribe needs to be on hand while your students are walking the course to record their guesses for how long it will take them to run the course. You can either draft your instructors, or mix the jobs up among your students, having them to do the jobs when another jump height is engaged in the game.

Talk to your students about the homework assignment you gave them last week. They should have figured out their dog's YPS and their own pace divisor. Tonight they'll get a chance to test both.

You don't have to use the suggested course. You can design another based on the space available to you. However, you should incorporate some of the challenges from the working sets.

How to Conduct the Class

Ideally, you will play the game once, then break down to do the training sets. Time permitting, you'll play the game a second time at the end of the class.

For a larger class it would be advisable to break the class into three smaller groups and use one group per jump in the exercise. You will want to demonstrate with one dog for the whole group first, then split the groups and rotate throughout to offer help and suggestions. This exercise will be the beginnings of the 180° turn from or toward the handler. Allow at least 15 minutes to be sure that each handler gets several repetitions of each direction.

Please note that although this week's lesson plan deals primarily with teaching the *Turn* command, students will be expected to draw on the previously learned *Get Out* command in some of the working sets.

Week 8: Progress Worksheet

Instructors: **Date:**

Handler and Dog	Present	Notes

GENERAL NOTES:

Week 8: Facility Layout

One square = 10'

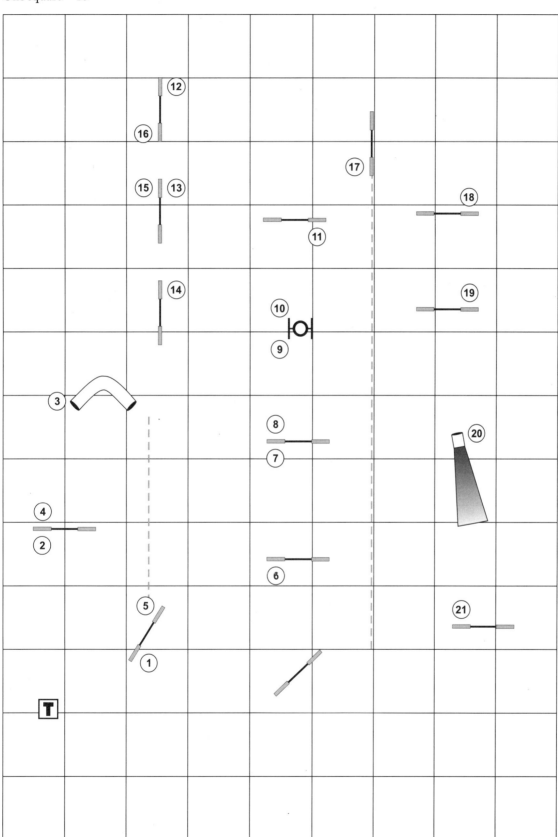

Week 8: Facility Layout Worksheet

Design your Facility Layout using a 1" = 10' scale (standard agility template)

WEEK 8

Week 8 Exercises: Timed Jumplers

This week's lesson plan deals with the issue of redirecting a dog. The ability to redirect a dog is often a must in more complex gambles. Redirection is a turn of 180° away from or toward the handler.

The redirection or *Turn* command as it will be referred to from here on, is a very helpful tool during the opening sequence as well as the joker portion of any Gamblers class. During the opening sequence it is often most efficient to do back-to-back same obstacle performance. Having the ability to issue a verbal command resulting in a tight 180° turn will save time and allow more points to be accumulated. In the closing sequence, or joker portion of the Gamblers class, the necessity of the *Turn* command becomes all too apparent.

For example, the dog is proceeding down a line of jumps, the next obstacle is positioned farther out than the rest. The dog turns in toward the handler. As the handler frantically shouts commands, the dog stares blankly back at the handler. The simple solution would be to give a *Turn* command, redirecting the dog toward the appropriate obstacle, then giving the command for the obstacle again.

The following working sets will allow you to help your students build an understanding of the *Turn* command. This lesson plan explores a few practical applications of the command. The initial teaching phase of the *Turn* command requires your students to use targets or a favorite toy, the latter being preferable.

Remind your students that the ultimate goal of this exercise, and the ultimate goal of the command, is to elicit a tight 180° turn. The efficiency of the turn should be monitored. You are looking for a pivot from the dog, essentially turning on his hindquarters.

Students should also be reminded that the *Turn* command requires a slightly delayed delivery when being used over a jump. If the command is given too early, dogs tend to drop their rear ends in an attempt to begin the turn, and may drop bars. The command should be given as the dog is landing rather than when he is in the air.

Set 1: Turn, Turn, Turn

These exercises lay the foundation for the negotiation of the *Turn* command. We will first work on teaching the dog to turn toward the handler upon completion of the jump. The next step will be to teach the dog to turn away from the handler and take the jump. Assign one group to each of the three jumps.

Send and Turn

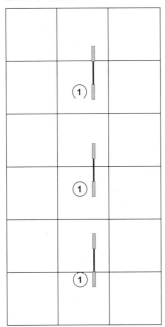

For the first exercise, instruct your students to do these steps.

1. Place the dog in a sit, stand, or down, facing the jump.

2. Command the dog to negotiate the jump. If the dog is hesitant to send over the jump a target with a favorite treat will be helpful for the first try or two.

3. As the dog completes the jump, take a step back while saying the dog's name and the command *Turn*. Follow with a *Jump* command once again (same jump, in the opposite direction).

Saying the dog's name is the attention-getting device that will begin to turn the dog. The *Turn* command immediately follows.

If the dog attempts to go around the jump rather than over it, it may be that the command was too early and the dog does not have enough room to make the turn and get over the jump. The dog might also run around the jump if the handler made a lateral movement as she gave the *Turn* command, instead of moving backward, thus pulling the dog around the jump.

As the dog begins to understand the game, eliminate the use of the dog's name prior to the *Turn* command. Expect the dog to turn on the verbal cue alone. This exercise is best worked with the handler varying her starting position on the starting side of the jump, with several repetitions for each new position.

Turning on the Flat

This step in teaching the *Turn* command is practiced without any obstacles at all. The purpose of this exercise is to teach the dog to turn away from his handler on the *Turn* command, using a favorite toy as a lure.

Instruct your students to follow these steps.

1. Armed with one of the dog's favorite toys, position the dog so that he is facing you.

2. Toss the toy behind the dog, while giving the *Turn* command. The dog will naturally follow the toy around, which should result in a smooth, tight 180° turn away from you.

3. Praise the dog immediately upon turning to get the toy and give the dog a short game.

Turn and Send

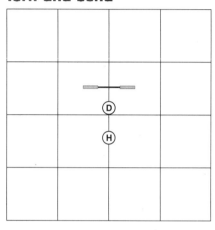

The next step will ask the dog to turn away from the handler to perform an obstacle. Instruct your students to get their dog's favorite toy or treat. A second person is also necessary if a target is to be used.

In this exercise, instruct your students to do these steps.

1. Armed with one of the dog's favorite toys, the handler should place the dog between herself and the jump. The dog should be facing the handler, tail to the jump.

2. Toss the toy behind the dog and over the jump, while giving the *Turn* command. The dog will naturally follow the toy around which should result in a smooth, tight 180° turn away from the handler.

3. Praise the dog immediately upon completion of the jump and give the dog a short game.

Monitor your students' throwing. Remind them that the desired behavior is a tight turn or pivot. The dog should not be encouraged unintentionally to go wide by an arcing release of the toy. If the dog has difficulty redirecting to the jump, a second person can be on the opposite side of the jump as the designated target person with the dog's favorite toy or treat. Several repetitions of this exercise will be beneficial to learning this behavior.

Keep in mind these exercise are for teaching the *Turn* command. Any questions or problems your students might have should be addressed at this point. The following sets are designed to practice the turn in active situations.

Roger Brucker

Set 2: More Turn, Turn, Turn

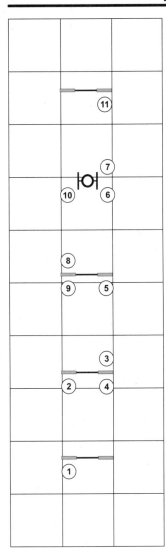

This set is designed to test the dog and handler's ability to execute the turn on the run. Although a working set has been designed for this exercise, do not hesitate to modify the existing set to add variety to the class. The set shows you just one of numerous possible combinations to enhance your dog's skills with the 180° turn. Included in the set are opportunities to turn away from and toward the handler.

This set would be fun to run as a timed event in class with top honors going to the dog and handler team who negotiates it the fastest. This would underscore the need for the dog to perform as efficient a turn as possible and test the handler's timing of the *Turn* command. Inappropriate timing will be obvious given the nature of the exercise and the potential speed of the dog.

Allow your students to walk the sequence and think through their timing. Run the set at least once, starting dogs on the handler's left side. Try it with and without a lead-out. Run more repetitions of the set running the dog on the handler's right side.

To set the game up, break the group of students into two smaller groups. Set jump heights to accommodate the smallest dog on the respective teams. Alternate one dog at a time from each team until all dogs have run. Add all team members' scores; the fastest team is the winner.

Note that the tire is used in this set. The tire features a smaller area for the dog to turn back and negotiate than on a jump. Remind your students that they will have to be aware of the dog's turning radius and adjust their handling position to aid the dog back through the aperture. A subtle *Get Out* command may be necessary if the dog takes a wide path around the tire. As the dog lands off the tire, the handler should give the *Turn* command as she takes a step back and turns away from the dog in the desired direction. If the dog attempts to come around the tire, the handler should give the *Get Out* command to move the dog off her side back to the center of the obstacle.

This will be a fairly time-consuming set that will most likely require 20-30 minutes of class time. Be sure to plan accordingly.

Set 3: Just Chute Me

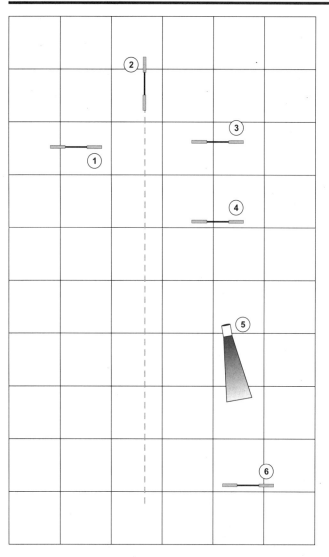

This set has the distinct feel and flavor of a typical NADAC-style gamble at the Open level. The ability to redirect the dog will greatly enhance the team's ability to meet the challenge of this gamble.

The chute poses the immediate problem. A chute is considered a blind obstacle due to the fact that the dog is unable to see the next obstacle or the handler during its performance. By adding the distance element, we are virtually begging the dog to come back to the handler upon completion of the chute.

A well-timed *Get Out* followed by the *Jump* command as the dog nears the end of the chute is necessary. However, most dogs will still suffer a sort of disorientation as they exit a blind obstacle. The natural reaction for the dog is to gravitate toward the handler indicating the need for a *Turn* command to the last jump.

Allow your students to give it a try the way they would normally handle a situation such as this. You will find that if the dog does indeed gravitate back to the handler, the most common response will be for the handler to hug the line and beg the dog to take the jump. If the dog is looking at the handler, the jump is no longer apparent to the dog and success is unlikely. The dog needs to be redirected toward the appropriate obstacle with the *Turn* command followed by the *Jump* command. It would be useful for the handler to move away from the dog while he is occupied in the chute, so that she can move forward, toward the dog, when the dog comes out.

Have your students try again, this time prepared to *turn* the dog if necessary. Remind them that in training the gamble line is merely a guideline. Success for the dog is the most important thing. If the dog appears confused, the hander should cross the line and help the dog. Another attempt at distance can be tried the next time.

As the dog enters the chute the handler should hang back a couple of feet from the exit. As the dog nears the end of the chute, the handler should give the verbal cues to *Get Out, Jump*. The handler should not move forward until the dog has exited the chute to ensure that the signal has registered with the dog. If the dog turns into the handler, the handler should hold her position and redirect the dog. The *Turn* command must be given from a stationary position to ensure the command does not get lost in the forward momentum.

This is a fairly complex exercise. Take care to avoid frustrating dogs or handlers. Be sure your students fully understand the dynamics of the exercise and are prepared to help the dog if necessary. The handler should step in immediately to direct the dog if the dog shows any sign of confusion. You will increase the dog's criteria for reward as he shows an increase in confidence.

Set 4: Push and Pull

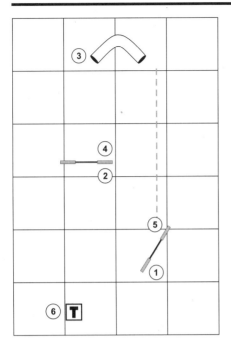

This is the most difficult of the working sets presented in this lesson plan. It requires a fair amount of natural impulsion from the dog and good timing from the handler.

This exercise exemplifies an Advanced or Masters level USDAA gamble. Redirection is part of the expected gamble. This is most evident in the push back from jump #5, which requires the dog to turn back to the table. A *Turn* command may also be required to get the dog from the tunnel at #3 to jump #4. Be prepared for this possibility.

Start by breaking the set into smaller exercises. The exercises can be worked from a stationary start or a moving start. The moving start will help provide impulsion for the less driven dog. Allow several repetitions of each of the following:

- Begin with the 1-2-3 combination.

- Do 3-4-5.

- Do 1-2-5-6.

- Do the entire sequence, #1 through #6.

Walk through these instructions with your students:

1. Start the dog at an angle providing a good view of jump #2 over jump #1

2. As the dog negotiates jump #1, give a *Get Out* command for jump #2 followed by a *Get Out* to the #3 tunnel.

3. As the dog exits the tunnel, face the dog and at the same time give a *Get Out, Jump* command. If the dog turns toward the handler, the *Turn* command should be used followed by the obstacle name.

4. Call the dog in over jump #5.

5. As the dog lands, give a *Come* command while taking a step forward. Follow this with a turn and send to the table.

Instruct your students to step in immediately to help out the dog if he shows any sign of confusion. Keep it positive and make success the ultimate goal!

Playing Timed Jumplers

This is a very simple game. The winner will be the team whose handler makes the closest guess as to how many seconds it will take her and her dog to negotiate the course shown in the Facility Layout.

Allow everyone to walk the course for ten minutes. No watches or stopwatches are allowed during the walk-though. The handler's guess must be based solely on *estimating* the dog's speed in negotiating the course.

At the end of the walk-through each handler must report to a scribe who will record the handler's guess on her respective scribe sheet. When the dog runs the course, the actual time on course will be subtracted from the guessed time.

Faults are added to the dog's running time so that the total score is time plus faults. You must tell the competitors what fault basis you are using prior to the walk-through since they may want to include an estimate of faults in their guess.

Week 8: Student Notes

Cherie Gessford

Now that you have come to the conclusion of your initial foray into serious distance training, it would be a good idea to consider the various situations that make distance training so important. There are certainly the obvious Gamblers classes. But your distance control and handling shouldn't stop there.

The importance of distance control on any Standard agility course must not be overlooked. This is what gives you the ability to be in those crucial handling positions when you need to be there. This is what allows you to keep up with even the fastest dog.

Distance is often the element that separates first place and second place.

Putting Your Distance Training to the Test

First let's explore the relevance of distance work in the Gamblers class. When you are planning the opening sequence of the Gamblers course, it is important to make use of your dog's distance skills in preparation of the closing sequence or gamble portion of the class. Planning an opening that includes both lateral distance and send distance will greatly enhance your chances for success after the whistle blows.

Practice pacing yourself to include subtle speed changes while directing your dog through the course. One of the biggest mistakes handlers make in the closing portion of the Gamblers class is screeching to a halt at the gamble line and sending the wrong information to the dog. The screech stop simply tells the dog to stop. You must prepare the dog to accept speed changes while working so that there is no misunderstanding between dog and handler as to what the expectations are.

During the Gamblers class walk-through, plan your strategy to include a set of obstacles that resembles the gamble sequence if possible. This serves to relax you more than educate the dog as to the impending gamble. However, this is a team effort. Both you and your dog need to be confident in your abilities. By staging a dress rehearsal you will be more relaxed heading to the line. It would also be beneficial to include a couple of back-to-back obstacle performances in your opening. It is often the case that even the most well-timed and thought-out closing sequences require at least one redirection of the dog. If a similar redirection has been practiced on the course, it increases once again the likelihood for success.

Where does distance training come into play for Standard classes? Lateral distance will allow you to maintain the shorter running path, compelling your dog to new speed to keep up. By using more direction and allowing the dog more independence on course, you will begin to see a dramatic improvement in your running times.

Your new working vocabulary—*Get Out* for lateral distance, *Go On* to keep your dog working ahead, and *Left* and *Right* direction cues—will help you attack any course challenge with confidence, and at full speed. You have spent a lot of time and energy training these various commands. Don't be afraid to use them.

The key to successful distance control and handling is the foundation that you lay for your dog at the onset of training. Continue to train and refine your distance working skills. It is never to late to teach a dog new skills. Consistency will always be your best training tool.

Putting It All Together

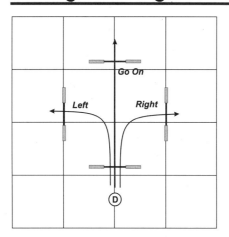

For Week 8 you will ask your dog to make the choice of left, right, or straight in the confines of a close jump square. Begin by closing in your jump square from Week 7 to make the distance between the four jumps universal.

This exercise is designed to test the attention capabilities of the dog as well as his *Left, Right,* and *Go On* proficiency.

1. Set up the dog behind the first jump.

2. Send the dog over the first jump.

3. As the dog commits to the jump, ask for either a *Left* or *Right* turn; or ask the dog to *Go On* straight. Then give a command for the appropriate following obstacle.

The dog should make the turn or go straight ignoring the obvious challenge of the jump directly in front or to the side of him.

This exercise can be worked in steps: First, lead out between the two desired jumps. Use a verbal and directional cue. Second, use the verbal and directional cue from behind the dog, stressing the distance element. Finally, send the dog over both jumps, using only verbal cues.

Any attempts by the dog to take the unintended jump should be met with an instant verbal *Wrong*. Allow the dog to think through the problem. Reward instantly upon successful completion. Keep in mind that success is the ultimate goal. Do not be afraid to help the dog through a trouble spot rather than allowing frustration to set in on the part of the dog or handler.

A suggestion for the number and type of repetitions for this exercise would be three left turns followed by a right turn; three rights followed by a left, or three straight sends followed by a turn. It is not advisable to switch from left to right, right to left, or straight to a turn with only one repetition as the dog tends to become patterned and quits thinking. By doing a few repetitions of one direction before switching, you are creating a semi-patterned response. You can test your dog's thinking and attention capabilities by then switching to the opposite side or asking the dog to go straight.

To keep confusion to a minimum it is advised to work primarily one direction or the other per session with this particular exercise. At the very least do the 3:1 repetition of one side, work on something else, and come back to this set for the three to one of the other direction.

Conversational Directionals

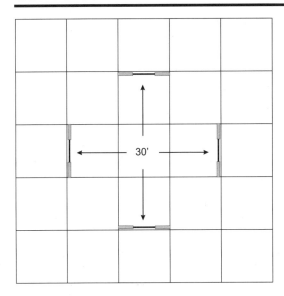

Here's a daily exercise for you and your distance-working pooch. All you need is four jumps and an area measuring no less than 50' by 50'.

The whole idea of this practice set is to provide you with object and actions for a conversational dialogue with your dog. Practicing a language is the way to develop facility with that language.

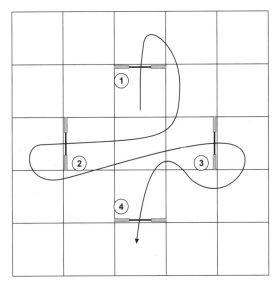

Here's how the training set works.

There are a lot of patterns you might use to sequence these jumps. Any that you might draw provide a foundation for dialog and training with your dog. You will work only the inside of the box, moving however much is necessary to keep the dog moving, directed to the correct jump, and turning in the desired direction.

The language is augmented only by movement (turns and forward motion) by you. So, how would this four-obstacle sequence go?

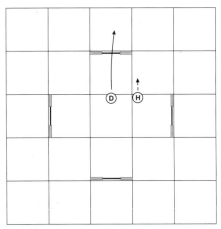

Handler: *Go... Jump.*

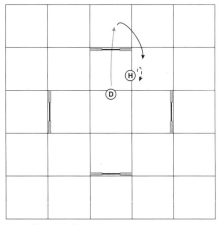

Handler: *Right... Come.*

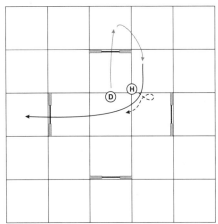

Handler: *Right... Go... Jump.*

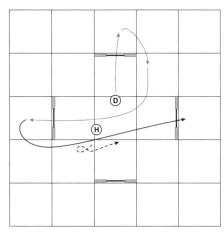

Handler: *Left... Come... Go... Jump.*

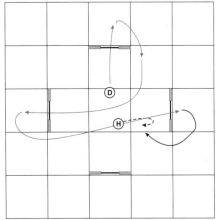

Handler: *Right... Come.*

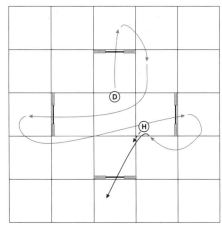

Handler: *Get Out... Jump.*

This is just a sample dialog. Remember that you must begin this work by moving with the dog as robustly as necessary until the dog learns to respond to the verbal cue alone.

When training a dog to work at a distance, you would ideally leave this setup in the backyard and work twice a day with different sequences. Don't make the sequences too long. Use play with a toy as a reward.

Go the Distance

Appendix

Turn! Turn! Turn!

Teaching the *Right* and *Left* Directional Commands

Lessons With Linda: Working With the Pill Bug

Gamble Scrambles

Jo Ann Mather

Go the Distance

by Linda Mecklenburg

A directional command that has a multitude of uses is the *Turn* command. The command is intended to direct the dog to turn around and go in the opposite direction. There are many instances where this type of directional control may prove useful on the course:

- Expediting repetition of an obstacle.

- Getting the dog to turn away from the handler.

- Effecting a change of sides.

- Expediting a turn.

Repetition of an Obstacle

Figure 1

Figure 1 shows the handler sending the dog away from him over the jump and commanding *Turn* to turn the dog back toward him to repeat the jump.

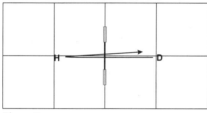

Figure 2

Figure 2 shows the handler calling the dog over the jump toward him and commanding *Turn* to turn the dog back away from him to repeat the jump.

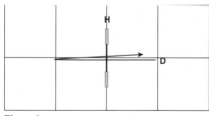

Figure 3

Figure 3 shows the handler sending the dog over the jump lateral to himself and commanding *Turn* to turn the dog back, still lateral, to repeat the jump.

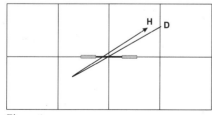

Figure 4

Figure 4 shows the handler sending the dog away from him over the jump and commanding *Turn* to turn the dog back toward him to repeat the jump.

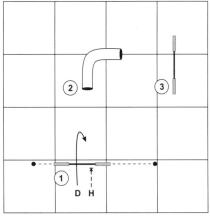

Figure 5

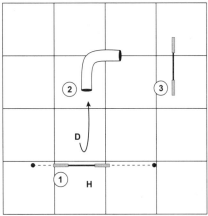

Figure 6

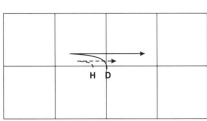

Figure 7

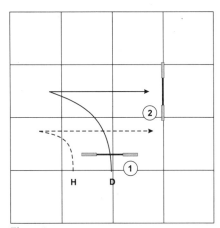

Figure 8

Turning Away from the Handler

As shown in Figure 5, if sent over a jump on a verbal command alone (as may occur during performance of a gamble), many dogs will turn back to face the handler. The handler must then point the dog at the correct obstacle before expecting the dog to perform it. Merely shouting *Tunnel* in this case is unlikely to be successful because the dog has its back to the tunnel and is looking at the handler.

The *Turn* command directs the dog to turn around and go in the opposite direction. In this case, once the dog is turned and the tunnel is within its field of view, a *Go Tunnel* command may now succeed as shown in Figure 6. Having a directional command that turns the dog back away from the handler so that it can be sent to a distant obstacle can be a valuable asset in Gamblers classes. Some handlers use the herding command *Look Back* for this purpose.

Change of Sides

Figure 7 shows the handler with the dog on his right side. The handler begins a turn to the left and allows the dog to pass in front of him, at which point the handler changes direction back to his right and commands *Turn* to the dog. The *Turn* command directs the dog to turn around and go in the opposite direction. The dog will now be on the handler's left side.

Figure 8 shows how the handler has used the same maneuver shown in Figure 7 to direct his dog from jump #1 to jump #2 with a change of sides. A handler may use the *Turn* command in this manner to effect a change of sides if he

- prefers not to cross behind (perhaps the dog is green or the dog knocks bars);

- feels the dog needs extra yardage between the two jumps; or

- feels the resulting approach lines the dog up for a succeeding #3 obstacle more effectively.

Go the Distance

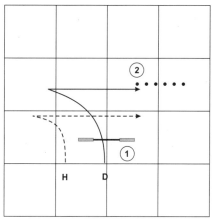

Figure 9

Figure 9 shows how the handler has used the same maneuver shown in Figure 7 to direct his dog from jump #1 to the weave poles with a change of sides. In this case, the handler uses the *Turn* command not only to allow him to work the dog from heel-side, but also to encourages a more controlled, straight-on approach to the poles rather than the random approach that would likely have resulted from a rear cross change of sides.

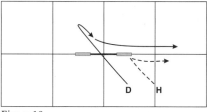

Figure 10

Figure 10 shows the handler with the dog on his left side. The dog and handler are approaching the jump from an angle right to left and the dog must turn right after the jump. The *Turn* command directs the dog to turn around and go in the opposite direction. In this case, as the dog turns it is redirected with a *Come* command and the handler's motion *before* it can repeat the obstacle. The result is a spin that is induced and controlled by the handler to expedite the turn and change of direction.

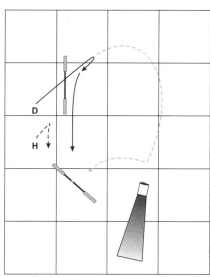

Figure 11

Without the *Turn* command, the dog will likely arc wide to the right as shown in Figure 11. Momentum propels the dog forward and makes it difficult for the dog to turn. The *Turn* command directs the dog to turn around and go in the opposite direction. In this case, as the dog turns, it is redirected with a *Come* command before it can repeat the obstacle. The *Turn* command has been used to effect a more efficient turn that does not arc wide, wasting time and presenting the dog with off-course possibilities.

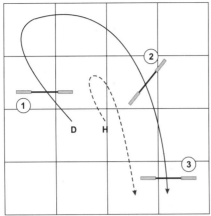

Figure 12

Placement of the succeeding obstacle on the course will often determine which type of turn is most beneficial. Figure 12 shows the #3 jump directly in line with the dog's expected path if it arcs wide after #2. There is no advantage to using a *Turn* command in this case.

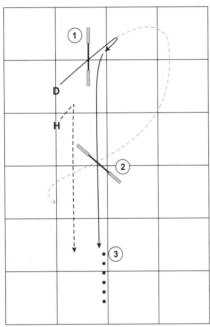

Figure 13

Figure 13 shows the #3 obstacle having a very difficult approach if the dog arcs wide while turning right after #1. Here the *Turn* command is used to effect a more efficient turn that does not arc wide.

Teaching the *Turn* Command

There are no hard and fast rules on how to teach the *Turn* command. Use your imagination. Here are several suggestions:

1. Begin with the dog facing you. Command *Turn* and toss the dog's favorite toy or food treat behind him so that he must turn and go in the opposite direction to get it.

2. Begin with the dog at your side. Command *Turn* and toss the dog's favorite toy or food treat behind him so that he must turn and go in the opposite direction to get it.

3. Begin with the dog at your side but 10' lateral to you. Command *Turn* and toss the dog's favorite toy or food treat behind him so that he must turn and go in the opposite direction to get it.

   NOTE: It is recommended that Steps 1, 2 and 3 *all* be performed (not just one) so that the dog learns the act of turning and going the opposite direction relative to his position—*not the handler's position.*

4. Begin with the dog at your side on leash. Command *Come* and walk forward, command *Turn* and about face. As you turn, switch the leash to the opposite hand so that the dog changes sides. Repeat with the dog beginning on both sides.

5. Begin with the dog facing you approximately 25' away. Command *Come* and recall the dog. As the dog nears you, command *Turn* and toss the dog's favorite toy or food treat behind him so that he must turn and go in the opposite direction to get it.

6. Begin with the dog at your side on leash. Command *Come* and run forward, command *Turn* and about face. Repeat. Praise and reward.

7. Begin with the dog facing you with a jump behind him. Command *Turn, Go Jump* and toss the dog's favorite toy or food treat behind him so that he must turn and go in the opposite direction, over the jump, to get it.

8. Begin with the dog at your side with a jump behind him. Command *Turn!, Go Jump!* and toss the dog's favorite toy or food treat behind him so that he must turn and go in the opposite direction, over the jump, to get it.

9. Begin with the dog at your side with a jump ahead of him. Command *Go Jump.* As the dog lands, command *Turn, Jump* and toss the dog's favorite toy or food treat behind him so that he must turn and go in the opposite direction, back over the jump, to get it.

10. Begin with the dog facing a jump and you standing at the wing. Command *Jump.* As the dog lands, command *Turn, Jump* and toss the dog's favorite toy or food treat behind him so that he must turn and go in the opposite direction, back over the jump, to get it.

    NOTE: With all steps, it is entirely permissible and even advisable with some dogs for the *handler* to *move* (turning with the dog and going in the intended direction) to cue the dog as to the expected action with body language. This is particularly true when the dog is first asked to turn away from the handler. Gradually, as the dog learns what action expected, the dog will perform the maneuver independent of the handler, on the verbal command alone.

Teaching the Right and Left Directional Commands

by Linda Mecklenburg

No discussion of the teaching of the *Right* and *Left* commands would be complete without first stating that the most important directional command in dog agility is *Come*. Nearly all agility courses can be run successfully using handler positioning and the *Come* command as the primary means of changing the dog's direction. However, the occasional course situation (such as Masters Gamblers) requires the dog to work independently of the handler. The *Come* command, which relies on changing the dog's direction relative to *the handler's position*, may not be adequate. The directional commands *Right* and *Left*, in which the change of direction is performed relative to *the dog*, are useful when the dog is working at a distance and has no handler as a reference point.

The available avenues for teaching the *Right* and *Left* directional commands to the dog are limitless. There is no single method. The step-by-step progression described here will result in the dog fully understanding how to change its direction based on the verbal directional command alone. Some dogs may benefit from using other techniques in conjunction with this one, in order to facilitate the dog's comprehension.

Many handlers have successfully taught *Right* and *Left* concurrently; however, I recommend teaching *one* of the directional commands and then the other. With the *Come* command, the dog easily learns that the expected response is to change direction dependent on the handler's position. With a *Right* or *Left* command, the dog must learn to change his direction independent of the handler. This is a difficult concept for the dog. It is preferable not to make it more complicated by combining the teaching of two different directions simultaneously. This forces the dog to not only learn the desired action, but to discriminate between the two directions as well.

To teach the directionals, the handler uses a motivator to induce the dog to move, and subsequently reward the dog for the action. The most common motivator is a ball or toy, but food can also be effective. I prefer to use dry kibble that has some weight, rolls, and is readily visible. I do my initial training indoors (usually from the Lazy Boy) where the kibble is easily seen, rather than outside in the grass. A food tube may also be used. If the dog is toy motivated but does not retrieve, use a Flexi lead to facilitate the return of the toy motivator to you.

First, follow Steps 1 through 7 to teach the dog to go right.

NOTE: Steps 1 through 4 can easily be taught to puppies.

Step 1: With Motivator

• The dog faces the handler.

• The motivator is held in front of the handler so that it's visible to the dog.

• The handler commands *Right* and simultaneously tosses the motivator 5' to 10' to the dog's right (the handler's left) as shown in Figure 1.

• Repeat the exercise several times. Perform short, frequent sessions each day—ultimately 100 to 1000 total repetitions. This is not an exaggeration. Ideally, the dog will, at some point, begin to anticipate and will demonstrate a desire to move right. The response the handler should expect is variable. It may be as subtle as a glance or a lean toward the right. Or, the dog may actually move to the right prior to the command. The dog is *not* required to move to its right before the motivator is tossed.

Step 2: Concealed Motivator

• The dog faces the handler.

• The motivator is held behind the handler so that it's *not* visible to the dog.

• The handler commands *Right* and simultaneously tosses the motivator 5' to 10' to the dog's right (the handler's left) as shown in Figure 1.

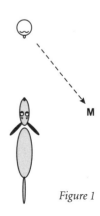

Figure 1

- Again, repeat the exercise several times. Perform short, frequent sessions each day—ultimately 100 to 1000 total repetitions. This is not an exaggeration. At some point, the dog will begin to anticipate and will demonstrate a desire to move right, but the response may be variable. As with Step 1, the response could be very subtle. Ideally, the dog will actually move to its right in response to the command, rather than waiting for the motivator to be tossed. However, the dog may not move to the right. The dog is *not* required to move to its right before the motivator is tossed.

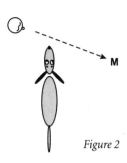

Figure 2

Step 3: Independent of Handler

In this step, the handler begins to change position relative *to the dog*. Until now, the dog has moved right relative *to the handler's* position. To help the dog understand that the desired action is independent of the handler's position, the handler must vary his position relative to the dog.

- The dog is left on a stay. The handler varies his position relative to the dog as illustrated in Figures 2 through 7.

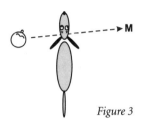

Figure 3

- The motivator is held in front of the handler.

- The handler commands *Right* and simultaneously tosses the motivator 5' to 10' feet to the dog's right, as shown in Figures 2 through 7. (Always be sure the motivator is tossed correctly, relative to the dog!) The motivator should be aimed so that the dog must turn a full 90°, or even more, to get it. The dog is *not* required to move to its right before the motivator is tossed.

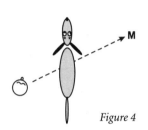

Figure 4

- Repeat the exercise several times from variable positions. Perform short, frequent sessions each day—ultimately repeating the exercise 100 to 1000 times. This is not an exaggeration.

Step 4: With Motion

In this step, the dog performs the direction change while in motion. Until now, the dog has been stationary when the *Right* command was given and the motivator tossed. To help the dog understand that the desired action can be performed while in motion, the dog is commanded *Right* while moving.

- The motivator is first held in front of the handler, visible to the dog, then behind the handler, not visible to the dog.

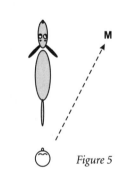

Figure 5

- The dog is left on a stay and then recalled toward the handler.

- The handler commands *Right* and simultaneously tosses the motivator 5' to 10' feet to the dog's right (the handler's left). The dog is *not* required to move to its right before the motivator is tossed.

- Repeat this exercise several times. Perform short, frequent sessions each day.

In the next exercise a send-away is used to get the dog in motion.

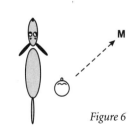

Figure 6

- The dog is sent on a go-out (assuming the dog understands a send-away). The dog can also be sent toward a table, to be redirected by the *Right* command.

- The handler commands *Right* and simultaneously tosses the motivator 5' to 10' to the dog's right. The dog is *not* required to move to its right before the motivator is tossed.

- Repeat this exercise several times. Perform short, frequent sessions each day.

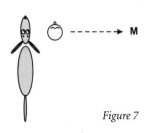

Figure 7

Step 5: With Obstacles

In this step, you will give the command in conjunction with agility obstacles for the first time. Until now, the dog has been asked to go *Right* independent of the agility obstacles. To help the dog incorporate the use of the directional command when on course, the handler must introduce its use in conjunction with the equipment.

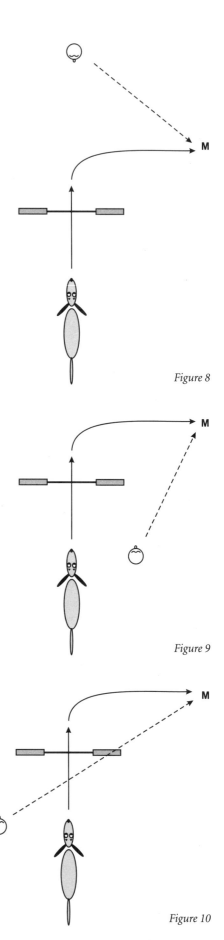

- The dog is left on a stay and then recalled toward the handler over a jump.

- The motivator is first held in front of the handler, visible to the dog; and then behind, *not* visible to the dog.

- The handler commands *Right* as the dog jumps, and simultaneously tosses the motivator 5' to 10' to the dog's right (the handler's left) as shown in Figure 8. The dog is *not* required to move to its right before the motivator is tossed.

- Repeat the exercise several times. Perform short, frequent sessions each day.

In the next exercise, the dog is sent over the jump from the handler's left side.

Figure 8

- The motivator is held in the handler's left hand.

- As before, the handler commands *Right* as the dog jumps, and simultaneously tosses the motivator 5' to 10' to the dog's right as shown in Figure 9. The dog is *not* required to move to its right before the motivator is tossed.

- Repeat the exercise several times. Perform short, frequent sessions each day.

In this next exercise, the dog is sent over the jump from the handler's right side.

- The motivator is held in the handler's left hand.

Figure 9

- Again, the handler commands *Right* as the dog jumps, but this time uses an airplane arm signal, simultaneously tossing the motivator 5' to 10' to the dog's right as shown in Figure 10. The dog is *not* required to move to its right before the motivator is tossed.

- Repeat the exercise several times. Perform short, frequent sessions each day. This exercise helps prepare the dog for cross behinds later on.

Figure 10

Go the Distance

Step 6: Change of Direction Between Obstacles

This will be the first actual use of the command to initiate a change of direction between agility obstacles. Until now, the *Right* command has been applied following the performance of a single obstacle. For the dog to respond to the command to change its direction between obstacles, the first sequence will be performed.

- Two winged jumps are placed at right angles to each other so that a right turn is required.

- The dog is sent over the first jump from the handler's left side.

- The handler commands *Right, Jump* as the dog jumps, and simultaneously tosses the motivator 5' to 10' beyond the second jump. Ideally, the dog turns to the right and jumps the second jump in order to reach the motivator. If not, assist the dog toward jump #2, using handler motion and a hand signal.

- Repeat the exercise several times. Perform short, frequent sessions each day.

In the next exercise the dog is recalled to the handler.

- The dog is left on a stay and is recalled toward the handler over the first jump.

- The handler commands *Right, Jump* as the dog jumps, and simultaneously tosses the motivator 5' to 10' beyond the second jump. Ideally, the dog turns to the right and jumps the second jump in order to reach the motivator. If not, assist the dog toward jump #2 with handler motion and a hand signal.

- Repeat the exercise several times. Perform short, frequent sessions each day.

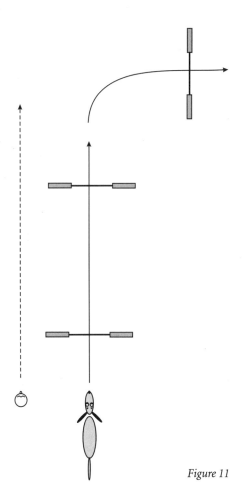

Figure 11

Step 7: The True Test

The dog is now ready for use of the *Right* command when running a course. In general, he will have body language cues to assist him. To test the dog's understanding of the *Right* command, set up the sequence shown in Figure 11. The handler should run with the dog over jumps #1 and #2, and command *Right Jump* for jump #3. If the dog complies and turns away from the handler to jump #3, the dog has demonstrated a clear understanding of the directional command. Congratulations!

Step 8: The Opposite Direction—Finally!

The teaching of the opposite directional command, *Left*, may now be undertaken beginning again with Step 1.

Until now, the process should have been limited to the *Right* command only. The concept of moving independently of the handler is difficult for most dogs to learn, and early progression is most likely very slow. Most dogs will learn the *Left* command in much less time. Once they understand the concept, equating the *Left* command with the appropriate action is simplified for the dog.

- As the *Left* command is taught, the *Right* command should only be practiced every third day, or so, and not in the same session as the *Left* command.

- When the dog demonstrates an understanding of the *Left* command, the two directional commands may be practiced alternately within the same practice session.

Lessons with Linda: Working with the Pill Bug

Observations by Bud Houston

The following sets were inspired by working with Linda Mecklenburg. The objective of the following exercises is to teach dogs to push out from the handler. These exercises are to be engaged at whatever pace the dog is reasonably capable of. It is always important not to push a training program faster than a dog can assimilate the new skills. As far as that goes, a handler should not move on before he or she is comfortable with the maneuver, lesson, or skill being learned. There is no hurry, after all.

A pill bug is the pipe tunnel curled around on itself to resemble one of those little armored bugs you can find in your garden or under the crawl space in your house. The pill bug is intended merely to be an imposing object which your dog must make a special effort to avoid. We'll use it here to teach the *Get Out* command.

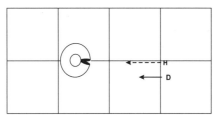

Figure 1

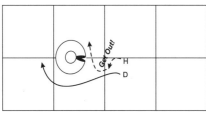

Figure 2

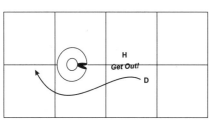

Figure 3

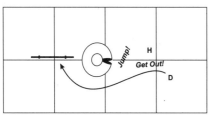

Figure 4

In Figure 1, the handler makes a direct approach to the pill bug with dog at side. Always approach the side on which the two ends of the tunnel are jammed together. It will be easier to keep the dog from trying to squirm into the tunnel if it is close to the handler, than it would be if the openings were on the far side of the pill bug.

The exercise is very much like the barrel exercise that we have described from time to time in the *Clean Run*. The barrel is an obstruction in the dog's path. Our intention is simply to send the dog around the obstruction without the handler having to resort to running around it himself. Figure 2 shows the basic maneuver. We will use this maneuver to teach the dog to *Get Out*.

The action of the handler is to: 1) Approach the obstruction with the dog at side; 2) Step into the dog, encroaching on the dog's path; 3) Give a hand signal (picture the hand on side of the dog, flicking out deftly); 4) Give the verbal command *Get Out*; and 5) Give the dog a reward and praise for getting out around the pillbug.

After several repetitions the dog will begin to anticipate the handler's action and skitter out around the pillbug with the voice command only. It is desirable to dispense with Step 2 (stepping into the dog). *Get Out* literally means get out away from me—take a wider path.

Figure 3 shows the handler maintaining a pretty much static position and using the *Get Out* to quickly alter the dog's path, out and away.

Once the dog understands the basic command, mix up the performance by pushing the dog out left, and pushing the dog out right, around the pillbug. Also alternate calling the dog in to the handler's side with *Come*, rather than pushing the dog out and away. Be very patient with this step so that the dog clearly understands what the handler means by *Get Out*. It doesn't hurt for the dog to have a pretty good idea what *Come* means either.

Now change the exercise by adding a jump as shown in Figure 4. The exercise is complicated to the extent that after the initial *Get Out* we add a command for the dog to *Jump*. The handler's timing needs to be good. As soon as the dog sees the tunnel, the handler should give the *Get Out* command.

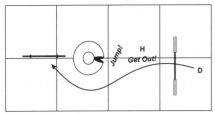

Figure 5

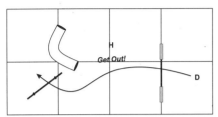

Figure 6

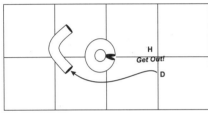

Figure 7

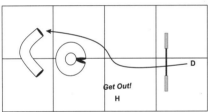

Figure 8

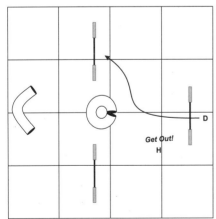

Figure 9

Next we begin the exercise with a starting jump to get the dog to approach the pillbug at speed as shown in Figure 5. The handler maintains the inside position, relying on a well-timed *Get Out* and then *Jump* when the dog first spies the jump on the opposite side of the pill bug.

The exercise is no problem for the dog. We simply have additional speed, making the handler's timing more important. But again, let's change the exercise, and present the opening of the tunnel to the dog. Now when the handler gives the *Get Out* command, it is to push the dog *away* from the possibility of entry to the tunnel as shown in Figure 6.

After several repetitions of this, begin alternating calling the dog, *Come* into the tunnel. When it is clear that the dog has learned and understands this exercise, we change the exercise again.

Now, rather than the jump, we put an additional tunnel behind the pill bug as shown in Figure 7. This is easier than a jump for most dogs in any case.

Next, add a jump to start the dog with some speed as shown in Figure 8.

In the next sequence, the pill bug is framed by two jumps as shown in Figure 9. To add some push, and distance, we put the second pipe tunnel out to capture the dog, and turn him back into the set. This also gives the handler the opportunity to add a new command to the working repertoire. Tell the dog *Go On*. (Affect a Cockney accent and say softly "Gowan then!"—that's the *rage* these days.)

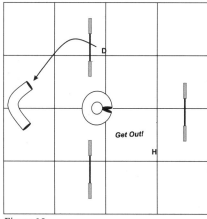
Figure 10

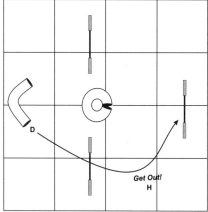
Figure 11

In this exercise, the handler learns to keep working his dog. Initially, the exercise is the same *Get Out* we've been doing all along. But we expect the dog to continue working away as shown in Figure 10.

After the second jump the dog might turn in short and lose the sequence. The handler's responsibility is to remind the dog to *Go On, Tunnel*, or if the dog really turns in sharp, the handler must push in with his body, and use a strong *Get Out* command.

As the dog enters the tunnel, the handler should fade back, into the path of the oncoming dog. He should then use the *Get Out* command for a brisk change of direction after the third jump, to the fourth and final jump as shown in Figure 11.

Use the last set to work both sides. Alternate working the *Get Out* command with working the *Come* command.

Go the Distance

GAMBLE SCRAMBLES

by Linda Mecklenburg

The following are sample gambles† for practice. For each equipment set-up, there are three potential gambles. Each set-up is designed to demonstrate a progression of difficulty from Beginner to Intermediate to Advanced with minimal equipment change. Most of the Beginner level gambles consist of variations of the jump-tunnel-jump theme. Challenge is then added by requiring one or more of the following:

- Performance of progressively more difficult obstacles such as the contact obstacles or weave poles

- The dog to be sent away from the handler more than once during the course of the gamble

- Obstacle discrimination

- Increased distance between dog and handler

- One or more changes of direction

Grids were intentionally omitted. Obviously the farther apart the obstacles are spaced, the more difficult the gambles become. Have fun.

† *Gambles* are sequences found in the USDAA and NADAC Gamblers classes where the handler is required to direct his dog at a distance. The handler's position is restricted to a designated area on the course. In the following diagrams the handler's position is generally behind the dashed line on the side *opposite* the obstacles.

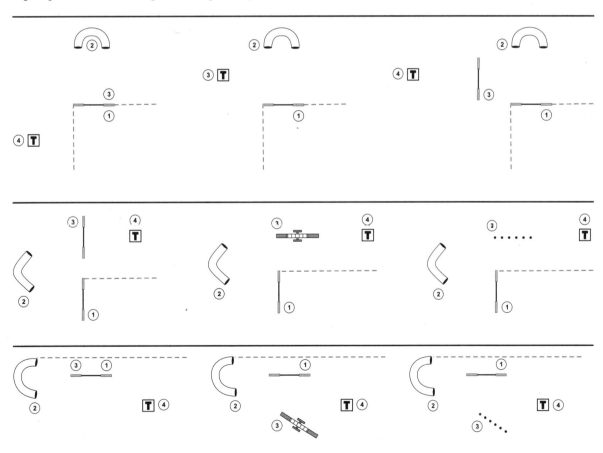

APPENDIX

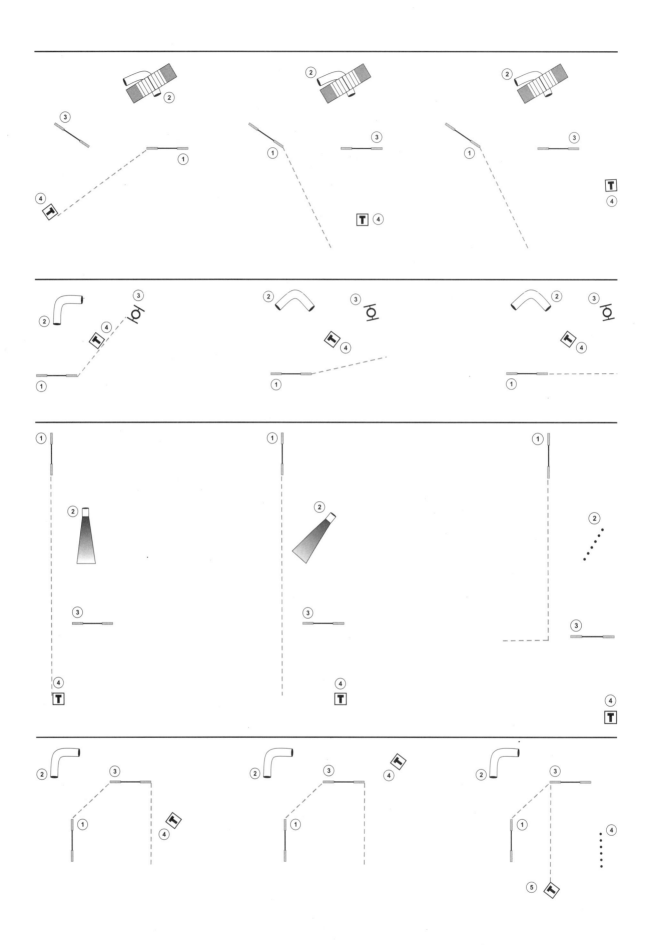

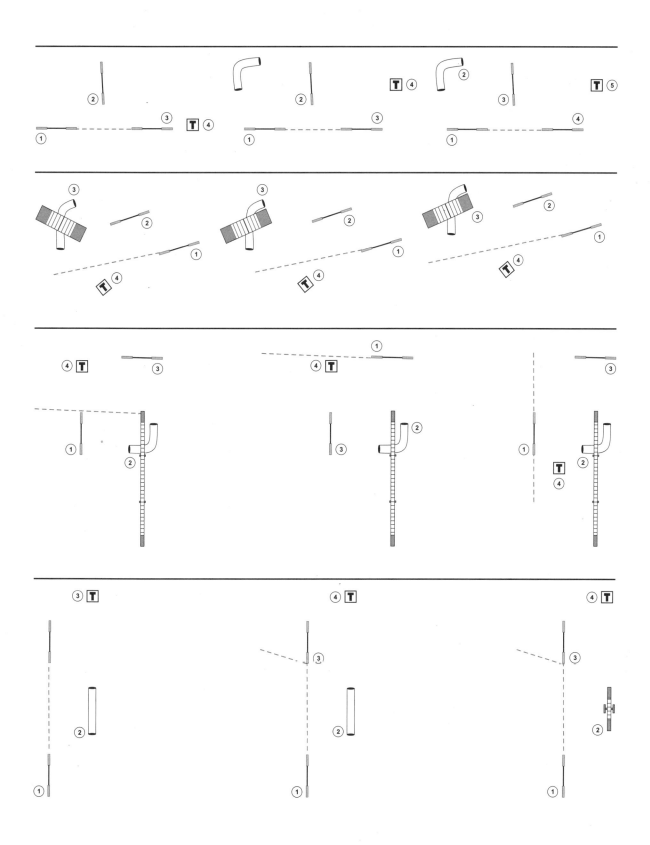

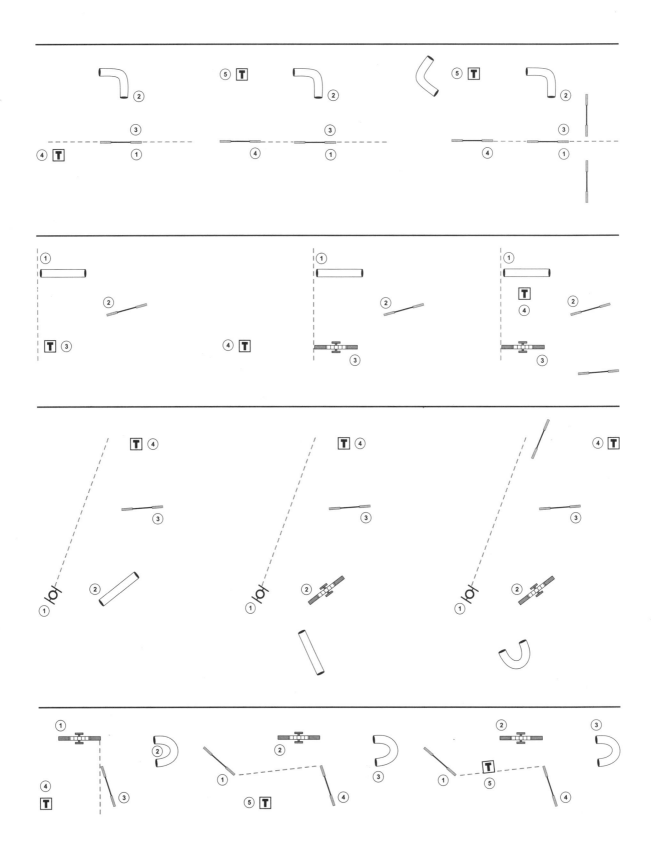

Go the Distance

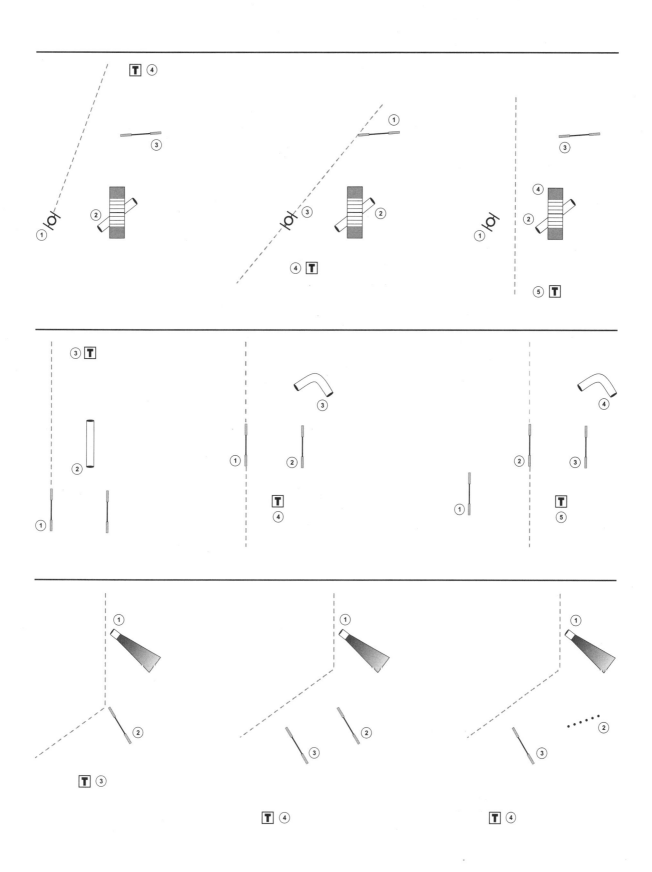

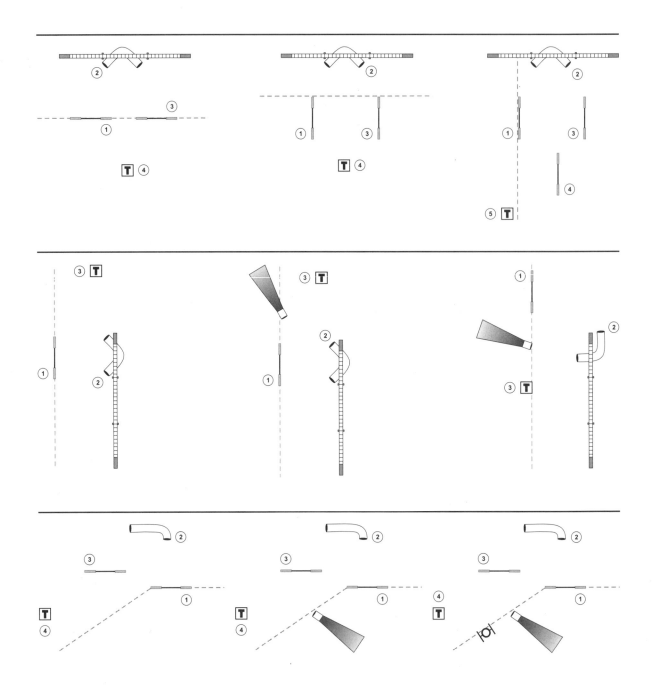

Glossary

This glossary contains several key agility terms along with *our* definitions of those terms. This should be given as a handout to your students.

Absolute directional: A directional command which directs the dog which way to move based on the dog's position, regardless of the handler's position; for example, *Left* and *Right,* which tell the dog to turn to its left or right, respectively.

Back: A command used to signal the side change during the execution of a rear cross.

Backchaining: Training method in which the last portion of an obstacle or obstacle sequence is taught first.

Centerline: The straight path the handler is attempting to take while the dog gets out laterally to perform the desired obstacle.

Come: A relative directional indicating that the dog should come toward the handler.

Containment line: This refers to a line, either drawn or physical in nature, that is intended to keep the handler from crossing into a certain area. It is a training aid in many instances when working on lateral distance.

Depressed angle jump: A jump that requires a dog to jump laterally over it. The approach to the obstacle is parallel rather than perpendicular.

Directional discrimination: A course challenge requiring the dog to be able to distinguish direction (that is, left, right, or straight).

Directionals: Any command given by the handler to turn the dog in a desired direction.

Food tube: A training device usually made of clear vinyl tubing that treats are placed in. The tube has either a slit in the side or end caps that come off which allow only the handler to get out treats for the dog. It is used as a target or can be thrown to aid in training the food-motivated dog.

Get Out: A relative directional instructing the dog to move away from the handler laterally.

Go On: A relative directional instructing the dog to go straight away from the handler.

Impulsion: A dog's forward speed or momentum toward obstacles.

Joker: The common name for the gamble or distance-handling portion of a Gamblers course.

Lateral distance: The distance that the dog maintains parallel to the handler.

Lead-hand cue: A signal given to the dog with the hand closest to the dog.

Lead-out: The dog is placed on a wait or stay at the start line and the handler moves out ahead of the dog prior to starting the course; or the handler moves into position for the next sequence while the dog is on the table.

Left: An absolute directional that tells the dog to turn to its left.

Micro-Managing: When the handler takes over the dog's responsibilities on course or in training, and tries to control every aspect of performance.

Neutral correction: To refrain from negative comment to the dog in regards to any given behavior. This is to signify to the dog that a different choice is required.

Obstacle discrimination: The dog's ability to recognize an obstacle and perform it by verbal cue. Also, a course challenge that requires the dog to discriminate between two obstacles, such as a tunnel under the A-frame.

Off-arm signal: An arm signal pointing the dog to an obstacle with the arm opposite the dog. Ostensibly, the off-arm signal bends the dog's path away from the handler.

Off-side handling: Situation where the handler is on the left side of the dog so that she is working the dog on the "non-heel" side.

Pinwheel: A configuration of three jumps in a classic "pinwheel" design.

Redirection: A turn of 180° away from or toward the handler that's often required in more complex jokers.

Relative directionals: A directional command that directs the dog which way to move based on the handler's position; for example, *Come* and *Get Out,* which refer to moving toward the handler and moving away laterally from the handler, respectively.

Reverse flow pivot (RFP): A maneuver used to shorten the dog's stride and pull the dog quickly into the handler as an aid in making a tight turn or grabbing the dog's attention before negotiating a challenge, such as an obstacle discrimination problem. The handler performs two pivots in quick succession, first turning into the dog and then turning back to the original direction.

Right: An absolute directional that tells the dog to turn to its right.

Send distance: The distance that a dog can be sent straight away from the handler.

Target: A training device, such as a paper plate, small square of Plexiglas, wash cloth, or plastic lid, used to focus a dog's attention forward or down to a specific area. The target is designed to give the dog an immediate reward for focus.

Thinking dog: The dog that is willing to try behaviors or problem solve. Your dog!

Threadle: An obstacle combination that requires the dog to perform one of two side-by-side obstacles, pass between the two obstacles, and then negotiate the second obstacle in the same direction as the first.

Turn: A relative directional that asks the dog to negotiate a 180° turn away from or toward the handler.

Verbal cue: Any command or cue indicated verbally by the handler.